Theodora, Empress of Byzantium

Empress

THEODORA

of Byzantium

CHARLES DIEHL

Translated by SAMUEL R. ROSENBAUM

FREDERICK UNGAR PUBLISHING CO.

NEW YORK

Translated from the original French
THÉODORA, IMPÉRATRICE DE BYZANCE
by arrangement with Editions E. de Boccard, Paris

CONTENTS

Translator's Foreword

By the third century A.D., the Roman Empire had spread from its base in Italy to include large areas in Balkan Europe, Asia Minor, Syria, Egypt, the North African Mediterranean provinces, and Spain, as well as what are now France and England.

Invasions by migrating hordes of hardy nomad tribes from the east and from the north had begun to penetrate its borders.

The Empire followed a pragmatic policy of encouraging settlements by such invaders. They replaced losses of indigenous populations, losses due to a variety of causes. The Empire was beginning to show symptoms of internal weakness. Rampant monetary inflation, luxury and corruption among the classes who controlled the government, were some of the ills that were sapping its strength. Production of foodstuffs in Italy itself was declining, so that there was increasing need to import foods and soldiers from remote provinces.

So-called barbarians were incorporated into the armed forces, eventually rising to positions of leadership in them and in the government itself.

By that time, the sources of wealth from which the Empire drew most of its necessities were principally in the East and across the Mediterranean, where the bulk of its real strength was centered.

Consequently, in A.D. 286, Emperor Diocletian, a Dalmatian by birth, divided the Roman Empire geographically in two for better efficiency of administration. He set up a capital in Nicomedia, on the Asiatic side of the Sea of Marmara, and from there he exercised personal control over the eastern half. He set up the western capital at Milan, removed from a Rome already in the grip of foreigners, and chose Maximian to rule from there as coemperor.

By the fourth century, Constantine had eliminated the double-throne system set up by Diocletian and had made himself master of both the Western Empire and the Eastern Empire after a series of internal military campaigns. He realized that the effective center of gravity of the whole Roman Empire was in the east rather than in the west. He selected for his capital the ancient Greek settlement Byzantium, on the European coast of the Bosporus strait connecting the Black Sea with the Aegean.

On this site he had a new city constructed and fortified, to which he gave the Greek name Constantinople. It was completed and formally dedicated in A.D. 330.

Ever since their conquest by Alexander the Great in the third century B.C., the language spoken by most of the inhabitants of Thrace (Constantinople occupied its eastern corner), Asia Minor, Syria, and Egypt, was a modified form of classic Greek. It was not long before the language of the imperial administration in the east in the fourth century A.D., as well as of the population generally, was almost entirely Greek, though the empire called itself Roman. Its citizens continued to refer to themselves as Romans.

Constantine and his successors claimed the right to rule over not only the provinces in the east, which they controlled directly, but also over what remained of the provinces in the west after the Gothic conquests.

During the fourth and fifth centuries, large portions of the Western Empire were seized and split off from it by Gothic invaders. Southern Italy became a fief of the Ostrogoths. Thus, Ravenna, in northern Italy, served as the western seat of the regime. Spain became an independent Visigothic kingdom. North Africa was invaded and seized by

Vandals migrating from Spain, and it rejected Roman domination.

Justinian (about A.D. 482–565) was born in Tauresium (commonly identified with the modern Küstendil) in Illyricum. He was brought up in Constantinople with a good classical Latin education. His uncle Justin, whom he succeeded as emperor in 527, was only a self-educated, partly literate but successful soldier.

Justinian's imperial policy was concentrated on his endeavors to recover for the empire the provinces it had lost in southern Italy, North Africa, and southern Spain. He hoped to renew the empire's dominance over all the lands surrounding the Mediterranean. He worshipped the culture of the Latins.

He married Theodora when he was nearly forty, after having been deeply infatuated with her for some years. Her early life was known to have been marred by the circus, in which she grew up. She was said to have been a woman of loose morals and a brilliant success as an entertainer and actress. She possessed great beauty, fascination, and native intelligence. She had great influence over Justinian and on his administration and the government of the empire.

While conducting his wars to recover lands in the west, Justinian was obliged to defend the empire from invasions by Persia to the east, and from incursions by Goths to the north. This involved him in immense expenditures for war and for the building of fortifications on distant borders. They drained his treasury continually and required ever increasing imposts on his subjects. One result was the Nika uprising described in this book.

Not the least of the problems with which Justinian had to cope was internal dissension caused by nationalistic movements in Syria and in Egypt. These were concealed behind religious differences within the hierarchy and among the communicants of the state-recognized Catholic church. Religious dissension was centered principally around the

Monophysite creed, a recondite, typically Greek philosophic reasoning that argued that Christ did not have two natures, one divine, the other human, but that he had only one, single nature.

Theodora was openly sympathetic to the Monophysite believers, possibly in part because she was convinced it was in the best interest of her husband and of the empire to avoid the secession of Syria and Egypt, where the monophysites were strong. Justinian, however, favored an effort to compromise with the Roman church and papacy. He wavered in his decisions, ultimately rejecting the eastern, Monophysitic orientation.

Parallel to the dissension in the church was the intense rivalry between the two factions calling themselves the Blues and the Greens. Originally, these groups were partisans in the audiences at the Hippodrome who favored one or another of the groups of performers there, especially among the racecourse charioteers. Their loyalty to their favorites was passionate, something like that of today's followers of favorite baseball or football teams. Gradually their feelings extended to favoring certain candidates and policies in political life as well.

The Blues tended to be the more prosperous and conservative citizens. The Greens were more of the working-class type, politically radical and, in religion, favoring the Monophysites. These factions were not actually political parties: neither had a well-formed program for political action. They served as an outlet for the expression of views and public opinion for or against governmental policies. They did not hesitate to voice their opinions violently while massed in the Hippodrome, where all athletic events, public sports, and large gatherings took place—the center of public life in Constantinople.

Charles Diehl (1859–1944), a respected scholar in France, became a leading authority on the history of the Byzantine Empire. He published this popular biography on the enigmatic Empress Theodora in 1904. The entire work has never before appeared in English translation, though a short abstract was published in English in a volume by Diehl, *Byzantine Empresses.*

In general, little has been taught about the history of Byzantium in history courses in the West. There is a growing interest in the subject today, probably owing to the current perception that the impulse of Soviet Russia toward world domination continues to reflect the maxim of the czars, "Moscow, the Third Rome." This was inherited from the Greek Catholic priest Philotheus, who first uttered these words after the fall of Constantinople to the Turks in 1453.

Some of the topical allusions in Diehl's book refer to events in Paris, where he lived, at the turn of the century. He intended his book for a popular, not a scholarly, audience. He refrained expressly from peppering his pages with footnotes or references to sources.

The chief source of first-hand knowledge of the period is the *Secret History,* written by Procopius, a disenchanted former secretary of Justinian. Diehl discounts much of the scandal retailed by Procopius, without intending to whitewash Theodora's reputation for having had a lurid past.

Diehl expressed sums of money in French francs and gold solidi. I have rendered his figures in the equivalent U.S. dollars of today.

—SAMUEL R. ROSENBAUM

Introduction

The experiences of Theodora, the Byzantine empress who rose from the backstage of the Hippodrome to the throne of the Caesars, have had a way, through all time, of stimulating the world's curiosity and exciting its imagination. During her lifetime her prodigious good fortune astonished her own contemporaries so vastly that the idlers of Constantinople invented the most incredible stories to account for it. Procopius methodically scooped up for posterity all that mess of prattle in his *Secret History*. After her death, Theodora became even more a figure of legend. People in the East and the West, Syrians, Byzantines, and Slavs, continued to vie with each other to embellish her romantic career with ever-more romantic yarns. Thanks to this lurid reputation, it is Theodora alone, among the many princesses who graced the throne of Byzantium, who remains well known and almost popular today.

More than one visitor to the Church of Saint Vitalis at Ravenna tries to decipher the enigma of Theodora's pale and immobile visage among the flickering golden mosaics in that solitary apse. In Paris, where only twenty years ago she trod the boards of the Théâtre Porte Saint Martin, or yesterday, as it were, when she appeared there again as if in an apotheosis, she aroused the curiosity equally of dramatists, of artists, of historians, and even of those who are usually indifferent to everything.

It may be, as Procopius quite maliciously reports, that respectable folk in Constantinople would carefully step aside and avoid Theodora if they encountered her in the

1

street, for fear of being soiled by contact with her impurity. In our generation, we no longer entertain such fears or such prejudices. On the contrary, the faint perfume of scandal that floats about Theodora rather attracts us to her.

One after the other, she has tempted the brush of a Benjamin Constant, haunted the creative imagination of a Victorien Sardou, allured the inspired fancy of a Sarah Bernhardt. Not very long ago, to bring her to life before our very eyes, all the splendors of a sumptuous stage setting were extravagantly lavished on a most faithful dramatic presentation. For a whole week it was the most fashionable tea-table chatter in Paris to debate Theodora's chastity.

Yet can we really say that we truly know this renowned empress, in whom so many see nothing more than an illustrious adventuress? And can we believe that, if she could speak, she would be entirely content with some of the splashy brushstrokes that have too often been added to ornament her portrait, today as of old? I am not quite sure. There are actually two Theodoras: she of the *Secret History*, and she of history without the adjective.

The former is the better known. But if one strips Theodora of the almost epic grandeur of corruption with which Procopius has surrounded her, her career was, in a certain sense, conventional. It is the story we have often heard of a dancer who, having lived to the full, looks at last for a durable establishment, and, having found a dependable man, settles down to marriage and religion. Her type is Virginia Cardinal as Ludovic Halevy has drawn her in the pages of his *The Cardinal Family*.

But the other, whom we know less, is exceptional and interesting in a totally different way. She was a great empress who occupied a distinguished place alongside Justinian and often played a decisive role in his government. She was a woman of superior mentality, of rare intelligence, of energetic willpower, a despotic and haughty creature, intense and violent, complex and often disconcerting, but always infinitely fascinating.

Having made that observation, I hasten to add that you must not suppose I experience a desire, bordering on paradox and contrary to all that is plausible, to paint here a Theodora who is entirely honest and completely virtuous. You will see that, though accompanying it with all prudent reservations, I have accorded ample space in this book to the colorful anecdotes in the *Secret History*. Far from refusing to give them credence, it seems to me that, on the contrary, if they are read with careful attention, they help to analyze the psychology of Theodora in the period of her stormy youth more completely than has ever been done before.

We must realize, however, that now we have other sources than the *Secret History*. Other documents, quite new to us, have been found, especially in recent years, that help us to fill in the outlines of the celebrated sovereign's image more completely.

Beyond the biography of Theodore, abbot of Chora and Theodora's own uncle, which was written by a pious monk in the ninth century and recently discovered, we have the *Lives of the Eastern Saints*, written near the middle of the sixth century by John, bishop of Ephesus and one of the empress's intimates. There are some unpublished fragments of the *History of the Church* by the same author, and the anonymous chronicle attributed to Zacharias of Mytilene. There are other works, equally contemporaneous, such as the biographies of the patriarch Severus and of the apostle of the Monophysites Jacob Baradaeus, translated from the Syriac manuscripts in which they had long slept forgotten, which illuminate in a most unexpected fashion the role Theodora played in the field of religious policy.

To these we can add other writings, in ancient times better known but rarely consulted, such as those of John Lydus or new fragments from Malalas, not to mention the imperial *Novellae*, the tiresome verbosity of which discouraged the industry of even Procopius himself, although they are full of relevant information. Fortunately for us, Procopius left still other writings than his *Secret History* that we can also examine.

From all of these, if we take the trouble to examine them with care, certain facts emerge that throw a different light on personalities of Justinian's era than that in which they are usually portrayed.

If I insist on this, it is not at all, I ask you to believe, for the fruitless satisfaction of making a useless parade of my erudition. You will find neither footnotes nor citations at the bottom of the pages of this book. It is essentially the colorful, anecdote-studded story of Theodora herself that I propose to write here.

But that story, though I am compelled to make it lively, and possibly amusing, is nonetheless true. I beg the reader to do me the favor of believing that every fact I report is founded on precise evidence, and that even the hypotheses I occasionally allow myself to advance can, if there be need, be scientifically demonstrated. For a more complete and detailed study of the epoch, I take the liberty of referring the reader to the larger work I have published under the title *Justinian and the Civilization of Byzantium in the Sixth Century* (Paris: Leroux, 1902).

In a word, it is not only the romance of Theodora that I wish to recite. Others have done that, and very brilliantly. But it seems to me that, by trying to reconstruct the succession of scenes through which she lived—the turbulent Hippodrome where she spent her tempestuous youth; the ceremonious and magnificent palace where she reigned in her ambitious maturity; the colorful but troubled church, for which she felt anxiety that filled her thoughts until her death in piety—by sketching the figures of the leading personalities who lived around her—of her husband, Justinian; of her favorites Peter Barsymes or Narses; of her confidante Antonina; of her adversaries John of Cappadocia or Belisarius; of her protégés Anthimus or Severus, John of Egypt or Jacob Baradaeus—we may bring back to life the enigmatic complex creature that Theodora was, in her authentic setting and in her historical reality.

No doubt there will always remain a residue of a past unknown and mysterious in the strange existence of an empress who had been a theater dancer, in a career so full of fluctuation and variety as that of a courtesan who became one of the most eminent of statesmen through her ambition and her intelligence. I do not at all flatter myself that I have been able to resolve all the uncertainties and dissipate all the obscurities.

However that may be, this truly superior woman, who, after having charmed an entire public, was able to conquer Justinian and to reign over a whole nation for twenty years, deserves to be known otherwise and better than only through the gossiping of a sour pamphleteer or questionable legends inspired by her scandalous celebrity.

Not that I would wish to be one more who tries to rehabilitate Theodora's reputation. The writing of history is an enterprise into which some error and some absurdity always enter. But to understand Theodora as she was, the much applauded actress, the famous courtesan, before becoming the absolute sovereign of the greatest empire of her time, makes one better able to apprehend all the colorful fascination she exerted on the unusual world in which she lived, all the potent interest that it holds for the study of that vanished society.

—CHARLES DIEHL

PART ONE

Theodora
the Dancer

I

Theodora's Beginnings

Toward the early years of the sixth century Theodora's notorious reputation as actress and dancer filled all Constantinople.

Where she came from was not too well known. Among later chroniclers, some claimed she was born in Cyprus, that burning and passionate land of Aphrodite; others, with more likelihood, credited Syria with being her birthplace. Wherever it may have been, Theodora was brought to Byzantium in her infancy by her own people. It was in Constantinople, the turbulent and corrupt capital of the Byzantine Empire, that she grew up and was schooled.

But by a quite remarkable working of atavism she preserved the impress and the love of the country of her origin all her life. While Justinian, born in the primitive mountain region of upper Macedonia, became a cultivated Roman, profoundly imbued with the Roman spirit, Theodora remained always a true Oriental, holding to all the ideas, the beliefs, and the prejudices of her race.

Hardly anything is known of the family into which she was born. Later legend fabricated an illustrious, or at least a presentable, genealogy for her, out of a kind of respect for the imperial rank to which she later elevated herself. It ascribed to her a well-placed and conservative senator as father. In fact, her origin seems to have been much humbler. Her father, if one may believe Procopius's *Secret History*, was a man in poor circumstances, Acacius by name, who was by profession a keeper of bears in the Hippodrome. Her mother was one of those managing females often found in the backstage world of the circus. Three daughters were born in this professional household: Comito, Theodora, and Anastasia. The second, the future empress, came into the world probably about the year A.D. 500.

The old regulars at the Hippodrome still remembered the circumstances in which Theodora made her first appearance there in public. Acacius had died, leaving his widow and his three daughters in great distress. The eldest was not yet seven. To hold onto the job the deceased, the sole breadwinner of the family, had occupied, the mother saw no better solution than to join up with another man who, succeeding her husband as the keeper of the bears, would assume simultaneously the burden of the bears and of her household.

The success of this strategy, however, required the assent of one Asterius, the principal stage manager of the Green faction, who had accepted a cash payment to favor another candidate. To overcome his obvious ill will, Theodora's mother believed she could interest the public in her cause. One day, when the audience had assembled at the circus, she appeared in the arena parading before her the three little girls garlanded with crowns of flowers and holding out their little hands in a gesture of supplication. The Greens were only amused by this touching plea. Happily, their rival faction, the Blues, always eager to steal a march on their adversaries, hurried to grant the prayer that their rivals had so heartlessly rejected. They offered the Acacius family employment equal to that which it had lost.

Such was the first contact of Theodora with the public that she was later to charm and then to govern. She never forgot the episode. She made the Greens bitterly expiate the insulting indifference with which they had once ignored her supplication as a child.

Thus Theodora grew up, with her sisters, under the watchful eye of a mother destitute of scruples, in the underworld that frequented the backstage of the Hippodrome, and here she found herself well prepared for the future that lay before her.

The widow of Acacius, a practical woman, seeing that her daughters were pretty, pushed them into the theater, one after the other. Comito led the way. She succeeded brilliantly. Theodora followed, and soon she was accompanying her elder sister on the boards, playing small parts such as a little lady's maid. She accompanied her also to worldly gatherings where the beauty of an actress was much appreciated. Mingling thus at an early age in the society of high livers who were thoroughly corrupt, she experienced in the promiscuity of the dressing rooms many unchaste contacts and indiscreet familiarities.

When, in her turn, she reached the age to come out on the stage alone, she logically sought her fortune where the rest of her family were also finding it.

Theodora was extremely pretty. Those who sang her praises assert that she possessed such rare and radiant beauty that it could not be adequately described in words or in works of art. Even her detractors admitted that, with her slight body, she displayed incomparable grace and that her charming face, with its smooth pale complexion, was lighted up by great eyes full of expression, of vivacity, and of sparkle.

Very little of this devastating charm, with which she was to make so many conquests, is conveyed by the official portrait of her that we see in the Church of Saint Vitalis at Ravenna. Under her long imperial cloak her figure seems too tall and too stiff. Her slender, delicate face, its oval thinned down, with her fine, straight nose, shows a gravity that is solemn, almost melancholy. Under the heavy diadem that conceals her forehead and the heavy wig that almost hides her raven hair, only one feature remains evident in that faded picture: it is the beautiful black eyes of which Procopius speaks that still illuminate and seem to devour the face, under the somber barrier of the brows that meet above them.

Consequently, if today you wish to get some idea of what Theodora's celebrated beauty was like in her prime, you have rather to look elsewhere, at portraits by modern painters such as a Clairin or, even more, by a Benjamin Constant, who have tried to recreate the magic of Theodora, and, happily inspired by the mosaic at Ravenna, have restored to that cold and motionless figure some of its vanished charm.

But Theodora had much more to her than her beauty. She was intelligent, witty, and amusing. She had the gift of mimicry of a born actor. This she exercised gayly at the expense of her fellow actresses. She had a pleasant and amusing turn of phrase that inseparably attached to her even the most inconstant of her adorers. She was not always kind; she never restrained her mockery from using words that hurt if they would draw a laugh. But when she wished to please, she knew how to turn on her irresistible power to charm.

Daring, audacious, and brazen, she never merely waited for admiration to come to her; she put herself out to provoke it or to encourage it, with shrewdness but carefree abandon. As, after all, she had little moral sense—one can hardly see where she could have acquired one—and, to top it all, an unquenchably amorous temperament, she succeeded fast, not only in the theater but out of it.

So she became an actress, but she had no wish, as did so many others, merely to play the flute and become a singer or a dancer. She liked better to appear in *tableaux vivants*, where she could display the unclothed beauty of which she was so very proud, and in pantomime that gave free play to her animation and her gift of comic mimicry.

Even the habitual idlers of Constantinople, quite accustomed to seeing such gifts on display, appreciated, they said, the audacity of the exhibitions she risked on stage and the ingenuity of the daringly immodest theatrical effects to which she resorted to arouse the attention of an audience. They applauded frantically when she presented herself to them more than three-quarters disrobed, offering her beautiful body to the exciting caresses of the trained birds in her act. They enjoyed as well the sprightly grace with which, in those slapstick pantomimes in which blows fall like hail, she knew how to dodge away and laugh back at the storm.

But Theodora's successes were prodigious above all in more intimate contacts. To use the tactful expression of Gibbon, the solemn historian, her charity was universal. She soon became much celebrated in Byzantium for her gay parties, the boldness of her talk, and the multitude of her lovers. She certainly won admiration more for her beauty than for her reserve.

Sometimes she had hardly come off the stage when she would pirouette backstage in the flimsiest of costumes, doing the motions of the belly dance for her companions and her delighted intimates. She was inordinately proud of the mastery she had over this form of exercise. Again, in relaxed moments at the end of wild parties she would strike the most unbelievable attitudes and engage in the most unbridled talk. Only the Greek frankness of Procopius can suffice to describe the ingenuity and knowledge she demonstrated in the pursuit of pleasure, dispensing her favors to any class, guests or servants, and not hesitating to descend to the latter if the former proved weary in the rooms above.

A Byzantine historian says she had a spirit of curiosity and was fertile with inventiveness. If we can depend in detail on the anecdotes in the *Secret History*, they show that such a reputation was amply justified. Suffice it to say that, if one took these intimate reports literally, Messalina would be, compared to Theodora, a woman of modest demeanor and almost conventional morals. It must be added that, before long, Theodora was so thoroughly compromised by such sport that decent people, encountering her in the street, would draw away from her for fear of being soiled by contact with such impurity, and that the mere fact of meeting her was considered a bad omen.

I do not know if Theodora worried much about public opinion, but she did experience one unpleasantness, in consequence of the way she continued to pursue her chosen career, that made her more watchful. In spite of the measures she took to avoid so vexatious an accident, she became pregnant, and all the efforts she made to rid herself of her unwanted offspring before its arrival proved unavailing. So she bore a son whom she named John, but she gave the embarrassing infant so cold a reception and complained so violently about the impediment it would be to her career that the father concluded it would be wiser to assume the care of the child himself. Because he was obliged to leave, at about that time, for Arabia, either as a civil servant or for other reasons, he thought it better to take his son with him than to leave him with Theodora. The child turned up at a later time and caused the empress some annoyance, but at the moment the courtesan in her was delighted to be rid of him.

But the lesson was lost on Theodora. We know with certainty that she also had a daughter whom she tended with more solicitude.

That was about the year 517. She was more than sixteen when, by her beauty, her wit, and her dedication to pleasure, she had become one of the bright stars in the Byzantine underworld.

2

Byzantine Diversions:
The Hippodrome

Early in the sixth century Constantinople, where Theodora got her dazzling start, was a city of unashamed corruption. Prostitution brazenly flaunted itself, houses of ill repute invaded the whole city and set themselves up even in the venerated shadow of churches and monasteries. To supply the pleasures of the capital, procurers traveled all over the empire to recruit unfortunates who were lured by flattering promises of lovely garments and gorgeous jewelry. Even children under ten became victims of these miserable creatures.

Many women, free or slave, succumbed to these solicitations. From then on, as prisoners of their corrupters, often even bound under contracts not to leave the occupation to which they were condemned, they filled Constantinople with their shameless lewdness. Degrading habits, unnatural vices, showed themselves in broad daylight. Constantinople was like Sodom. Pious souls, who feared the just anger of the Lord, were as disturbed over the prevailing impiety and blasphemy as they were over the frenzy for gambling. Gaming went on everywhere, day and night, in public and private places. Huge sums were wagered and fortunes swallowed up. The evil was so general that even churchmen were affected by it. There were priests who frequented gaming houses, casting avaricious eyes on the gold pieces that were tossed about, defiling their hands, their eyes, and their ears. But the Hippodrome, and above all the theater, was the great school of corruption.

Justinian said: "Spectacles are necessary for amusing

the populace." So one of the great concerns of the government was to supply perpetual food for popular curiosity by
the glitter of ceremonies and celebrations. Chariot races,
hunting down animals, combats between men and ferocious
beasts, theatrical shows among which the public loved most
of all the farces, ballets and pantomimes, acrobatic displays
and the drolleries of clowns, followed each other endlessly
for the pleasure of the multitude. An uninterrupted week of
celebrations marked the beginning of the New Year; one of
the days bore the strange but significant title Prostitutes
Day. Without end, new splendors summoned the rabble to
the theater or the circus. Justinian never found a better
device for winning the favor of the crowd than making
twenty lions or twenty leopards fight in the amphitheater at
once, or awarding richly caparisoned horses to the winners
of horse races, or offering the populace a prodigious feast
and expending on it over $12,000,000 in three days.

All Constantinople frequented the theater or the Hippodrome, the gilded youth as well as the plebeians, priests
as well as laymen. And although custom forbade decent
women to be seen there, they were just as excited, even at a
distance, as their husbands about everything touching on
races, horses, and drivers. There never was a nation, not
even the original Roman people, more completely bound up
in the Hippodrome events than the Byzantines of the sixth
century.

The winning drivers became kings of the day. The emperor himself added to his own glory by praising them in
person. The administration raised statues to them, the
bright spirits of the capital taxed their ingenuity to celebrate
the winners' stunning victories in little verses. The most
serious thinkers declared that without them life would be
joyless. The multitude took sides and shared in the excitement according to the color of their caps. Greens and Blues
in turn, over the years, felt their honor was at stake, as
though the issue were the saving of the country from danger.

As may well be imagined, an enormous personnel was involved in organizing such games. There had to be poets to compose the verses in which, on their respective days, the factions would sing to do honor to the emperor; composers to set these to music; organists to accompany them; conductors to direct them. There had to be ushers to maintain order at the circus; guards to take down the barriers when the audience was to leave; checkers at the coatrooms to protect the caps and the golden crowns of the drivers. There were dancers, mimes, acrobats, jugglers for the intermissions; guards at the stables, keepers for the beasts, costumers and dressers. All these people swarmed backstage and around the Hippodrome, obviously a very mixed company among whom a number of adventurers and fast livers slipped in, hoping to find there some occasion for pleasure or profit.

Because the best society of the capital counted it an honor to belong to one or the other of the two principal factions as though to a kind of jockey club that had for its main purpose the production of the races, the very elegant world was also present backstage at the circus, strangely mixed together with that shady underworld crowd of drivers, clowns, procurers, and prostitutes.

The circus was the constant subject of sophisticated conversation. All Constantinople favored the popular driver or the fashionable actress and laid bets on approaching races. Even the most sedate gentlemen were not averse to discussing the origins of the games learnedly, as well as those of the colors of the drivers. They researched the symbolic meaning of these in order to settle the prophetic significance that the victory of either party would imply. Everybody knew that Green symbolized the earth, so that its triumph forecast a fertile year, and that the Blue symbolized the sea, so the success of that color foretold successes at sea. Naturally, therefore, the cultivators favored the Green, but sailors the Blue.

The circus was the inspiration of fashion. Young elegants who frequented the Hippodrome adopted an eccentric civilian costume to distinguish them from common people. They wore their beards untrimmed and their moustaches extra long, like Persians. Like Huns, they shaved off their hair in front and let it fall in long curls to the shoulder in back. They rolled up the sleeves of their jackets very tight at the wrist and had them cut extra loose at the shoulders, flattering themselves that this gave the illusion that they had robust biceps and doubly strong muscles when, at the theater or the circus, they raised their arms to applaud. They put on breeches and boots in the Hun style, with wide cloaks richly embroidered. So rigged out, wearing a short double-edged sword at the waist, they would cruise around Constantinople at night, molesting and attacking law-abiding passers-by, despoiling them of their jewelry and their garments and sometimes even assassinating them if they gave signs of resistance.

The Blues party, in favor at court since the death of Emperor Anastasius brought in a new dynasty to succeed him, was the first to make these amiable diversions fashionable. As neither the police nor the law courts would intervene to stop these misdeeds, of which the Greens, as opponents of the government, were generally the victims, the impunity enjoyed by the malefactors encouraged all the cutpurses and marauders in the dregs of the capital. At last the Greens, being constantly mistreated and never protected, organized protective gangs on their own to defend themselves. Order and security disappeared from the streets of Constantinople.

Soon peaceable people did not dare to go out at night. The rich, to avoid being attacked, wore imitation jewelry and shabby clothes. Nevertheless, terror reigned. Then nobody bothered to ask whether it was the Greens or the Blues who were to blame. Debtors took advantage of the disorders to claim they had paid off their creditors, slaves to free themselves from their masters, sons to extract cash from their fathers, lovers to rid themselves of their mistresses, and spendthrifts to satisfy their whims. Was there some enemy to be rid of? It was easy to find a cutthroat for pay. People were being killed even in churches during a service, and very often without even knowing why. It became a sport in the highest taste, and to be able to strike down an undefended man with one single blow passed as a proof of courage and strength.

Because the police, whenever they tried to take action, never struck at anyone but the Greens, and the magistrates likewise, in fear of their lives if they failed to observe the standing of the Blues, all equity was disregarded and incidents multiplied each day.

One day, at one of the wharves in Byzantium, a young woman was embarking with her husband to cross to the Asian shore. Some young men, noting that she was pretty, chased her boat and, having caught up with it, forced her to change over to theirs. The husband protested in vain. He got only hoots in reply. To save her honor, the unhappy woman saw no choice but to leap into the Bosporus under the eyes of her desperate but helpless husband. She drowned. The factions were responsible for other equally tragic occurrences, in which the survivors were never able to get justice.

It would have required great courage for officials to take action against such lawbreakers, protected as they were by powerful influences at court. Theodotus, the prefect of the city, experienced a sample of these influences, at his own cost.

There was one Hypatius, a highly placed personage, who had been assassinated inside the Church of Saint Sophia. The city was greatly upset over this. At that same time Justinian's nephew, the usual defender of the Blues, lay seriously ill. In these exceptional circumstances the complainants made their way into the presence of the emperor. He ordered the prefect to punish the crime with severity. The order did not have to be repeated. Theodotus at once had a number of the malefactors arrested and some of them executed. Among those executed was Theodosius Tzicca, a very rich man of high degree.

This is what undid the prefect. Justinian's nephew, who recovered as if by a miracle, thought of nothing but avenging his friends. By the nephew's influence at court Theodotus was accused in the senate of the most slanderous calumnies, deprived of his fortune, exiled to Jerusalem, and in the end forced to take refuge in a monastery to escape the daggers of assassins intent on his death.

This is how the quarrels of the Hippodrome factions created a state of terrible agitation in the city, which, some years later, was to lead to an actual uprising.

Meanwhile astrologers and mountebanks, fortunetellers, soothsayers, and rumor mongers found it easy to disturb the equilibrium of the capital, mental and moral. One day, at the Golden Gate a woman, in a paroxysm of prophesying, announced that in three days the sea, overleaping its shores, would submerge the whole universe under a new deluge. The populace, in panic, flocked into the churches and, prostrating itself at the foot of the altars, awaited the terrible catastrophe in consternation.

At other times astrologers read the approach of impending cataclysms in the stars. Soothsayers, misguided, ran through the streets as though pursued by invisible phantoms, warning horror-stricken passers-by that the end of the world was near.

And the folk, giving credence to such words, filled the basilicas with their prayers and their lamentations. Some entered convents, renouncing their positions and their wealth. Others offered their possessions to churches and spent their substance on works of charity. Each wished to perish in a state of grace. Sometimes the confusion persisted for weeks while the emperor found no way to still the terror, which he shared in as well.

Actually there were some sensible people who did believe that these agitators who troubled the capital with their impostures should have been arrested without further ado. But superstition was deep-seated and credulity universal. Women, as was to be expected, were particularly credulous of miracles. To hold their husbands or keep their lovers, they had less confidence in their beauty or their seductiveness than in magic potions and incantations.

In this, as in all else, Theodora was a child of her time. With her good friends Indaro and Chrysomallo she made up charms and miracle-working beverages that were supposed to assure her of having eternal and diabolical power over her suitors. She believed in demons, in magicians, in fortune-tellers, and in interpreters of dreams. Confident of her own future, she awaited her destiny with composure.

3
Theodora's Adventures

Theodora loved pleasure. She loved money, too. She had piled up quite a tidy fortune when she suffered a regrettable stroke of bad luck. She had a lover from Syria, Hecebolus by name, who held a position of some consequence in the imperial administration. He was appointed governor of the Pentapolis in Africa. Theodora decided to accompany him to that remote outpost. Probably it was at that time that she first made up her mind to put a stop to her temporary, passing affairs and to establish a more dependable connection.

Unhappily for her, the romance did not prove lasting. We have not been told just why, but before long the lovers quarreled. Hecebolus put Theodora out with violent abuse and no cash. Lacking means of any kind, the unfortunate girl, we are told, dragged her misery all over the East. She was seen at Alexandria, at Antioch, and elsewhere, following her tragic though lucrative profession by necessity in order to live. It was as though, to use the almost naively ponderous expression of Procopius, the devil wished to make certain that no part of the world should remain ignorant of her shamelessness.

It seems, however, that her long stay in Egypt at that time and in Syria made a certain impression on her character that was indelible and quite opposite to that one would have expected.

At that time Alexandria was not only a great commercial center, from which traders voyaged as far as Ceylon to bring back silks from China, as well as spices and precious stones from India. It was a gigantic marketplace from which grain from the Nile valley and the products of the Middle East were distributed all around the Mediterranean. In consequence it was not only rich and elegant—it was also content and corrupted. It was a land chosen by courtesans such as Thais and Chrysis, who became famous there.

Since the fourth century, however, the capital of Egypt was also one of the chief centers of Christianity. Nowhere had the conflicts in religious argument been more bitter, the theological disputes more acute and ardent, fanaticism more excitable. The memory of the great founders of monastic life, such as Anthony, Serapion, and others, had produced a wealth of mystics, hermits, and monasteries. The surroundings of Alexandria were studded with monasteries. The Libyan desert was so dotted with solitary hermits that it had earned the name of the Desert of the Saints.

At the time Theodora was there, Egypt was more disturbed than ever. It was during the reign of Emperor Justin, who, wishing to reestablish the union with Rome, was unloosing the most atrocious persecution of dissenters. All in the Byzantine Empire who refused to adhere to the orthodox beliefs proclaimed by the Council of Chalcedon—those who, like Eutyches, claimed that Jesus possessed only a single nature and were, for that reason, known as Monophysites—were mercilessly beaten down.

The most illustrious leaders of that sect, such as Severus, the patriarch of Antioch, Julian of Halicarnassus, John of Tella, Peter of Apamaeus, and more than fifty other bishops, had been driven from their bishoprics, anathematized, and sent into exile. In Syria the monastic communities had been scattered by force, their monasteries closed down, and the monks put to flight by violent measures, imprisoned, or massacred.

Many of the victims of these actions had sought safety in Egypt, where the patriarch Timothy, confident in the steadfastness of his army of fanatically devoted monks, remained faithful to the Monophysite doctrine. Severus had taken refuge in Alexandria. As the most remarkable of the leaders of the sect, he was known as "the Rock of Christ, the immovable guardian of the true faith." By his fiery sermons and the ardor of his convictions, he maintained a powerful agitation all over the Eastern world.

Men of noble birth and women of elegant and refined background, burning with religious fervor and an overpowering desire for solitude, asceticism, and renunciation, had been resorting for years to caves in the Libyan mountains and to monasteries lost in the depths of the desert in search of health and forgetfulness.

Saint Thomas was one who belonged to a distinguished family. He had been raised like a child of royalty. He had large means, wealth, crowds of servants. The naive chronicler who celebrated Thomas's sainthood says he was so addicted to ceremony that he would wash his hands and face more than ten times a day.

When the winds of persecution began to whistle through Syria Saint Thomas followed Maras, the holy bishop of Amida, into Egypt. To earn his keep this great gentleman worked with his hands, weaving baskets out of palm leaves, which he sold. To assure his eternal salvation this man of fashion wished to become dead to the world. He lived for years in the cave he chose for his retreat, mortifying his flesh, perpetually praying and bemoaning his sins. Finally, burned by the sun and withered, his whole body turned black. His long hair fell in shaggy disorder to his shoulders. He was dressed in filthy rags. Even his friends could hardly recognize him. But Thomas was happy. "What does it matter," he would say, "if this mortal body goes to ruin, provided that my soul, defiled by so much sin, escapes the eternal fire at this price?"

Caesaria was another patrician of high degree, related to the family of Emperor Anastasius. She, too, had left her home and her possessions to go to Alexandria and live in retreat. This cultivated woman of luxury and splendor edified all the world by her piety and the austerities she practiced. She abstained even from eating bread. She contented herself with eating only every other day raw vegetables, coarsely seasoned with salt and vinegar, and a few grapes. She slept unclothed on a sack spread on the ground. Even her priests criticized the excess of her self-torture. They endeavored sometimes, on a Sunday, to add a little oil to her diet by making her fear that illness would too soon render her incapable of fulfilling her religious duties. But Caesaria would reply, "I only wish that God would grant that my body be ill all of my life, provided my soul might so be saved," and she persisted in doing her penance. Well educated, she read the writings of the Fathers day and night, eagerly debating questions of dogma and belief humbly with the most lowly of monks, anxious to hear from their mouths an echo of the word of God.

Above all, Caesaria's ambition was to flee the world, to live in the desert. She grieved greatly when her advisers objected to her doing so because of her age and the weakness of her body. During fifteen years she was a marvel to Alexandria with her piety, her charitable works, and her humility. She wanted to be the lowliest of the sisters in the convent she founded, giving all an example of modesty and of self-sacrifice.

Many others lived like that as well. The hermit Maras was early won over to asceticism, fasting, praying far into the night without respite, allowing his body only an hour or, at most, two for rest. When the snow reached almost to the height of a man, he went out in it barefoot to cut firewood on the mountainside. He could be followed by the footprints marked by the blood that flowed from his wounds. At the end he avoided the pleas of his own people, went off to Egypt, and, sitting at the feet of the most celebrated solitaries to learn from them, aroused universal admiration by the holiness of his ways.

Women were matchless beyond all. Saint Susannah refused the most ordinary food, asking only that she be brought a little bread every other day and a jug of water every Sunday. She spent years in the desert, waging dreadful struggles against demons. In these struggles she was always victorious to such a degree that they were convinced she was not a woman at all and had a stone in place of a heart and iron in place of flesh. Her countenance always hidden by veils, which left hardly more than the point of her nose visible, she wished neither to see any human face nor to subject anyone to temptation. To all who came to visit her she spoke of the weakness of the flesh, the vanity of the world, the threat of the terrifying judgment of the Lord. She tended the bodies and comforted the spirits, uplifting the courage of her neighbor hermits, giving them strength by the example of her womanly fortitude and moral fervor.

Pious pilgrims came from all over to the Desert of the Saints to ask the ascetics' advice, their prayers and their blessings, renewing their own zeal by witnessing the austerities they practiced and discussing the holy mysteries with them. Others betook themselves to Severus, the exiled patriarch of Antioch, whose theological knowledge and eloquence were universally celebrated. Women especially were impressed by the irresistible power of his sermons. The patrician Caesaria was one of the penitents whose conduct was molded by his advice.

In the deep misery that then depressed her, Theodora was greatly influenced by the atmosphere into which the events in her life had projected her. During her stay in Alexandria she consulted the patriarch Timothy. The bishop seems to have had a profound effect on her. Later she was to call him her spiritual father. In view of her reserving that title for him alone, one can speculate with good reason on whether the repentant courtesan had not been reborn, at least for the time being, into a life less impure and more Christian thanks to this priest.

Theodora also visited Severus of Antioch. There is no

doubt that the depth of knowledge of religious questions, of which she was later to give so much proof, was acquired in the lessons she received from him. In any case she cherished a loyal and respectful attachment, as well as unbounded admiration, for the great Monophysite doctor all her life.

If she appeared at first to be the natural protector of the persecuted dissidents, the empress "raised up by God" (to quote one of her contemporaries) "to shelter the afflicted against the fury of the tempest"; if she placed her influence at the service of Severus and his friends, receiving them at the palace, favoring the dissemination of their ideas, striving to impose them on Justinian; if she threw herself ardently into the theological controversies of her day—it was not solely, as we shall see, for reasons of state policy or because of a very balanced and perceptive understanding of the needs of the government. It was doubtlessly also caused by her memory of the moral crisis she had gone through in Alexandria, by her lively gratitude to the men who had received, taught, and lifted up the lost courtesan.

But Theodora was a woman, and consequently changeable as well as vehement. She was also ambitious and eager to repair the state of her fortunes. In that vast Syrian city Antioch, where she went when she left Egypt, she found that the taste for spectacles, the love of luxury and of well-being, the endless rivalries of the theater and the circus, were the regular pattern of life. She seems to have frequented the backstage of the Hippodrome more than the churches, and the society of fortunetellers more than that of priests. Macedonia, a dancer who, like Theodora, belonged to the faction of the Blues, took an interest in her, offered her consolation in her distress, and assured her that she was destined to enjoy a brilliant future. Theodora allowed herself to be lulled by these hopes. At night she would dream that when she got back to Constantinople she would become the favorite of the Prince of Demons, succeed in marrying him and after that in having all the riches in the world.

It seems that the good Macedonia knew Justinian and

had done him services that gave her some standing at court. Did she make use of her influence to recommend her friend Theodora to the heir presumptive of the empire? I do not know. In any case it seems that when she returned to Byzantium, the scene of her first successes, Theodora was a wiser and more settled woman, weary of her wayward life and her madcap adventures, possibly also hoping to concentrate on achieving a secure establishment and applying herself, sincerely or not, to leading the quietest and most respectable life possible.

According to a tradition still current in the capital in the eleventh century, on her return from Asia Theodora lived correctly and modestly in a little cottage, keeping house and weaving wool, like a matron in the good old Roman days. The legend adds that later, when she had become the empress, far from wishing to obliterate the memory of that part of her life, Theodora wished, on the contrary, to perpetuate it. She had a church built in honor of Saint Pantaleimon at the site of the portico of the cottage that had sheltered her when, humble and poor, she earned her living by weaving. The name of the saint in Greek signifies "the Merciful." He deserves that title if it was to his protection that Theodora owed her introduction to Justinian.

4
Theodora and Justinian

When Justinian met Theodora, probably about 522
A.D., the future master of the Byzantine Empire was a man
of about thirty-eight or forty. With his light, healthy complexion, his long, curly hair and his slender moustache already tinged with gray, his elegant figure and slim waist, he
had a very attractive appearance. His obliging manner, his
amiable and melodious voice, and the simple grace of his
bearing made him sympathetic and fascinating. He was well-
bred and extremely rich. Apart from all this, thanks to the
palace intrigue that had raised his uncle Justin to the
throne, he was at that moment one of the leading personalities of the state. Clothed in such titles as count and patrician,
commander-in-chief of the garrison troops, he had just completed with extraordinary brilliance a tour of duty as consul.
Each day the good will of the sovereign brought him closer
to the steps of the throne. He was a wonderful conquest for
Theodora to make.

Ambitious and capable, Justinian seemed to be concentrating on advancing his fortunes. He had the skill to push
aside rivals who might impede his progress, even if some
deception were necessary. With equal adroitness he knew
how to win the favor of all classes of Byzantine society.
Very religious and strictly orthodox, he was well regarded
by the church. By his pomp and his prodigal generosity he
was the idol of the multitude. Finally, he was approved by
the senate and the aristocracy.

Because, with all this, he had had some actual experience in matters of state, had a prodigious capacity for work,

and paid careful attention to administrative detail, his standing was of the highest with the emperor. He really merited, better than did the elderly but mediocre sovereign, the title of head of the government. Very smooth, with apparently complete self-control and an iron will, he appeared to be entirely mature and his character completely developed. It was this earnest and serious statesman, this politician and diplomat, who fell madly in love with Theodora.

Their intimacy, which was to culminate in marriage, struck their contemporaries as so surprising and astonishing that, to explain it, they could attribute it only to miracles, to philters and the power of magic that Theodora must have practiced on her lover. But in fact, it was not at all necessary to make it as complex as that. Justinian was said to have an extremely amorous nature. Behind a very positive exterior he concealed an indecisive and vacillating spirit, easily subdued by the strong, energetic will of another.

Theodora was pretty and remarkably intelligent. She moved with easy grace. She displayed the pleasing and witty sense of humor that enslaved her most fickle adorers. Most of all, she had a logical, firm mentality. Everybody testifies that her nature was positive, authoritarian, and vehement. From the first moment the prince was completely smitten. Until the day Theodora died Justinian remained true to the boundless passion for her that she had kindled in him when she was young.

As a historian of the period put it, she was for him "the sweetest charmer of all." He himself was pleased to pun on her name, describing her as "his gift from God." Loving her to distraction, he could refuse her nothing she ever asked. She was greedy for honors and recognition. Playing on the weakness of his uncle, Justinian had her elevated to the peerage as a patrician. She was ambitious, avid for power. He let her sit in his councils, made himself the docile tool of her preferences and her prejudices. Ever since her youth in the Hippodrome she had tenaciously harbored her grudge against the faction of the Greens. To please her, Justinian made her the protectress of the Blues, even in face of the offense this was to public opinion. From her wanderings, from her stay in Alexandria, she had preserved a touching partiality for the persecuted Monophysites. To indulge her, Justinian even agreed to relax the rigor of his orthodoxy and to extend some tolerance for these stubborn dissidents.

This personal attachment of the heir to the throne soon became a matter of public knowledge. Shortly, outside the capital itself, in the remote provinces of Syria and Egypt, it was learned, no doubt with astonishment, that the little courtesan of earlier days, the penitent of Timothy and of Severus, had become a patrician and was the recognized mistress of Justinian. Pious Monophysites saw in this unexpected development the hand of God, anxious to provide a faithful protectress for His flock. Quite naturally they appealed to Theodora to ease the lot of the martyrs and to mitigate the rigors of the persecution. She lent an ear very willingly. Maras, bishop of Amida, with his priests, had been deported to Petra. In the harsh climate of Arabia, in the primitive conditions of their exile, these unhappy creatures seemed doomed to certain death.

In their misery they dreamed of Theodora. One of them, the deacon Stephen, made the trip to Constantinople to interest her in the fate of the little community. Their hope proved to be well founded.

Not only did she agree in person to persuade her orthodox lover to solicit the emperor's favor on behalf of these dissidents, but she herself spared neither prayers nor tears to prepare to aid in procuring Justin's assent. It was therefore not so remarkable that she won the case to which she had lent such strong support. Her followers were authorized to return to Alexandria, or at least to live in peace thereafter surrounded by their own coreligionists. It was a splendid victory and indicated the measure of the influence Theodora exercised over her lover.

She was to do even better. Before too long, Justinian reached the point where he had made up his mind to marry his mistress against all opposition. Good Emperor Justin had no wish to haggle over giving his much-loved nephew his assent or to do so with poor grace.

Justin was an old soldier of humble origin, not impressed by the quarterings of the upper classes. Not long before, he himself had wedded a former slave, after having for a long time paraded her in his train as his mistress whenever he visited the encampments of his troops. He showed no hesitancy in seating this woman, equally as rustic and barbarian as himself, beside him on the throne of the Caesars.

It was not from him but from a wholly different and unexpected source that opposition to Justinian's plans arose. To the earthy, peasant common sense of Empress Euphemia (the very elegant name that had been given the former slave who became empress), it was shocking to see a woman like Theodora succeed her. In spite of her affection for her nephew and her usual willingness to comply with his every wish, she would hear none of it. Fortunately for Justinian, Euphemia died soon after, in 523 A.D. Then all was arranged without further trouble.

The existing law forbade senators and other high dignitaries to marry women whose status was that of servants, daughters of innkeepers, actresses, or courtesans. To please his nephew Justin abrogated this law. Wishing, as he put it, to imitate the mercy of God, who showed mercy for every mortal sin, he decided that any woman who had been on the stage but had repented of it and quit her dishonorable profession could afterward enter into a legitimate marriage with anyone at all, on the sole condition that she apply for an imperial authorization to do so. As this rather limited concession might offend Theodora's pride, it was further stipulated that every comic actress who had been granted recognition by the council of state would, by reason of that fact alone, be relieved of every legal impediment to her marriage with any man of certain specified ranks. She would consequently not be required to apply for any special permission to marry him. To complete the removal of all such barriers, the emperor added at the end of his decree that daughters of such actresses (Theodora having a daughter) who had been born after or before their mother's act of repentance would likewise be free to marry without the slightest restriction.

Justinian then proceeded to marry his mistress. This was in 523 or 524 A.D. He took advantage of the occasion to settle a handsome dowry on her.

Byzantine society cautiously refrained from showing any sense of being scandalized by this. A few who had been hoping to promote a fine marriage of the heir to the throne to a certain well-educated, young, and innocent noblewoman were chagrined, though they were careful not to protest too vocally or to point out that this indulgence of Justinian was a measure of his good judgment and his sense of public morals. Neither the senate, the army, nor the church uttered a word of protest publicly, and the public, who remembered having lavishly applauded Theodora as an actress, now poured out their homage and their affection on her as their sovereign.

From that time on she officially shared the life of the prince. Old Justin, who seems to have developed great affection for her, admired her immensely. Theodora took a hand in the affairs of state more boldly every day. In spite of her many shortcomings she had one rare characteristic: she never wavered in her loyalty to those she liked. The Monophysites learned this by experience early.

Sensing the danger the monarchy would be in if pointless religious quarrels were allowed to continue in the East, she cleverly manipulated her standing at court to lay plans to put an end to the formal persecutions. She maintained contacts with the patriarch Severus and with the great heretic preacher John of Tella. She saw to it that she met the influential leaders among the dissenting Christians who seemed to be capable of planning a better future for their brethren.

One of the best known of these was Jacob Baradaeus, the future apostle and restorer of the Monophysite church. He was extolled for his knowledge of the sciences, his piety, the austerity of his daily life, his scorn of all things of this world, and the miraculous cures he could effect even at a distance. There was already a marvelous halo about the figure of this young Syrian monk. Theodora wanted to meet him. It was reported that she had seen him in a dream holding in his hands golden vessels from which he let fresh water run to slake the thirst of the Roman people. She decided to see him in reality.

Consequently, about 527 A.D. Jacob proceeded to Constantinople in the company of another monk, Sergius of Tella. The renown of his glory had preceded him. The populace followed his every step. Theodora was delighted that he had come. She received him and his companion with great pomp. She turned over a house for their residence, provided them with everything they would need, and covered them openly with the mantle of her protection. It took great audacity to risk the fury of her orthodox court by such actions, but Theodora felt her power and knew it was constantly growing.

After his marriage Justinian himself was also growing in public esteem. Justin raised his nephew's status to that of *nobilissimus*. In April 527, Justin associated him formally with himself as coruler. The old emperor mounted his throne in the great Triclinium of the palace and, in the presence of the senate, the garrison, the guards, and representatives of the army, he announced that by request of his people, he had elevated his nephew Justinian to the rank of basileus, emperor. Standing at the right of the emperor, the patriarch Epiphaneus intoned solemn prayers, to which the entire assemblage piously responded *Amen.* Then Justin personally placed the crown on the head of his imperial associate while the whole audience shouted three great cheers and the new ruler, saluting his people by a gesture, promised the soldiers a generous donation, as was the custom.

Three days later, in the Church of Saint Sophia gleaming with lighted tapers, the patriarch solemnly consecrated the new emperor and anointed him with holy oil. In this burst of royal pomp Justinian took possession of the throne he had so long wished for, clothed in the golden tunic bordered with a wide band of precious embroidery, his feet shod in the boots of imperial purple, his waist girdled by the rich belt sparkling with glittering enamels and precious stones, wearing over his shoulders the great purple mantle enriched with woven gold and held by a golden clasp, on his head the diadem bearing all the crown jewels.

By his side, garbed in her long cloak of purple velvet, at the bottom of which a wide band of gold was woven into its luminous folds, her hair dressed with showers of pearls and precious stones that dripped about her shoulders in dazzling cascades, her diadem on her head, Theodora, embellished like an icon, shared the triumph of her husband. After having been crowned together with him in the basilica, the new Augusta went, as prescribed for Byzantine sovereigns, to receive the plaudits of the multitude in the Hippodrome that had long before witnessed her first public success. Her dream was realized.

A few months later, 1 August 527, Justin died. Justinian met with no difficulty in stepping into his inheritance, and Theodora shared Justinian's power with him. For twenty-one years, from 527 to 548, she continued to reign as the sovereign mistress over the most magnificent empire the civilized world had yet known.

5
The Theodora Legend

Such was Theodora's romance. Procopius tells the story. Ever since the manuscript of his *Secret History* was found, some two and a half centuries ago, his generally scandalous recitation has met with almost universal acceptance. But does this mean that every word in it must be believed? In recent years reliable writers have, on a number of occasions, questioned the reliability of this mess of gossip, so that now we can discuss what may be called the Theodora legend more dispassionately.

We can ask ourselves with good reason why, if Theodora had lived so dissolute a life in the public eye as to scandalize Constantinople, not a single witness among her contemporaries has come forward who remembered it. For it is evident that, outside Procopius, not one writer of the sixth century, not one historian of that or later centuries, has spoken of Theodora's checkered youth or ventured even the most discreet allusion to the flood of scandal that Procopius said was current. If it be claimed that this prudent silence can be attributed to respect for the emperor or to fear of the empress's vengeance, many of the authors, especially the ecclesiastical writers, would nevertheless not hesitate to overwhelm with abuse a sovereign whose heresy they hated, and to weight her name down with every possible malediction.

Even supposing that the mouths of her contemporaries were stopped by fear, why were their tongues not loosened after the deaths of both Justinian and Theodora? And, if this is the case, then, in the face of the prevailing silence, how much is the testimony of Procopius worth as an accusing witness, especially if one considers the almost naive effrontery with which, on so many pages of the *Secret History*, he may have distorted the facts or actually lied?

If, before becoming empress, Theodora had actually been so notorious a courtesan as he charged, how is it that there is no other echo, even muffled, of the outcry that he claims was so open and general about her? How is it that there is not a single derogatory word about Theodora in the chronicle of that unforgettable scene in 532 when the mob rioted against the many bloody outrages charged to Justinian, if one opens it to consult the record of the unprecedented debate between the ruler and his subjects?

And, finally, how can one explain that Justinian, a man known even to his detractors for his self-control and strength of mind, no longer a juvenile capable of committing rash imprudences when he met Theodora, could risk his popularity, even possibly his chance to succeed to the throne, not, mark you, by taking Theodora as his mistress but actually by publicly marrying her, a woman from whom decent people would turn away if they met her in the street?

However fair these queries may seem to sound, and however strongly I challenge the blather of Procopius, nevertheless I would not wish in the least to be accused of trying to wash clean a reputation he blackened so outrageously, and even if, since the sixth century, there have been panegyrists who, to flatter the memory of Justinian, would have us believe that his wife entered straightway into paradise, I would hesitate to commit the paradox of making her out as excessively virtuous.

It is regrettable that John, bishop of Ephesus, who was close to Theodora and knew her well, failed, out of respect for the great ones of the earth, to mention at length the charges of wrongs committed by the empress that pious monks, often men of rude frankness, heaped upon her. At any rate it is certain that among her contemporaries in the imperial household others besides Procopius, such as her secretary Priscus or the prefect John of Cappadocia, must have been aware of her vulnerable weak points, to which they at least could have pointed.

I do not know if in her youth she really had the son that Procopius attributes to her, whose birth was, as he says, such an unwelcome mischance. It is clear, however, that she did have a daughter who was not Justinian's and who might have served to recall a troubled past, but who, to judge by the success of Theodora's grandson at court, was no embarrassment to the empress or burden to the emperor.

In addition, there are some traits in Theodora's psychology that do accord with what has been written about her early career. Among these are the solicitude she displayed for poor girls in the capital who were led astray more often by poverty than by vice, the measures she took to redeem these unfortunates and to free them, as one writer of the day put it, "from the bondage of their shameful slavery," and the harshness, amounting almost to contempt, with which she usually treated men. If all this, which is undeniable, is admitted, must we not suspect that we cannot totally reject all the contents of the *Secret History*?

Certainly it is a delicate question, and one embarrassing to solve in any event, to try to determine just how far Theodora fell and to just what depths of infamy she sank. There are two comments that may help us a little to approach the truth and to clear up some obscurities in the story. One is that many things that strike us today as being shocking and scandalous were regarded by people in the sixth century as being infinitely less reprehensible. In one official document of the period we read that quite decent people did not hesitate at all but regarded it as simple charity to pay for obtaining the release of unfortunate sick girls from a house of ill repute, and later to see them married in a conventional ceremony in spite of the manner in which they had definitely been compromised. It seems that public opinion then was more disposed to admire than to criticize actions having a kindly purpose that might seem to us today to be overly delicate. It is conceivable that against such a background Justinian might have been able to marry Theodora without astonishing or scandalizing his contemporaries too violently. On the other hand, it is certain that Theodora, from the moment she met her last lover, mended her ways completely. During her stay in Alexandria she had gone through a moral crisis. Under the influence of pious instructors she had repented of her lurid past. On her return to Constantinople she remained quite poor. This in itself would tend to make us believe that she also remained virtuous.

In a great capital a great courtesan is quickly forgotten. After two years out of the limelight who would remember that she had been previously Justinian's mistress? After all, if you observe the predilections of Procopius and the epic depth of perversity he was apt to ascribe to his characters, you are disposed, without wishing to make of Theodora a model of virtue and chastity, merely to transpose the tune of the *Secret History* down a key or two. Then you see in Theodora, in place of a courtesan in the grand manner and an absolute spirit of evil who, carrying out the will of the devil, as Procopius says, exposes her shamelessness to all the world, only the heroine (even if on a diminished scale) of a much more commonplace story. It is then the story of a woman who was led astray more by circumstances than by vice; of a little dancer who, though she led the sort of life those of her kind in every age lead, decided one day to leave behind her the daily love affairs and, having found a man of substance who would assure her a permanent home, took marriage and religion seriously; of an adventuress, if you insist, but one intelligent, discreet, and shrewd enough to preserve appearances, one who could marry even a future emperor without creating an uproar of scandal.

However it may have started, the stroke of luck that

seated Theodora on the throne moved the popular imagination profoundly. During her lifetime her incredible fortune astonished many of her contemporaries beyond description. After her death her legend fed on itself to grow even greater. People of the East and the West, Syrians, Byzantines, and Slavs vied with each other to ornament her romantic story with ever-more romantic details, so that it has come down to us embellished and transformed from century to century, by turns indulgent or critical, as the fabulous legend of the wife of Emperor Justinian.

Ever since the ninth century, Byzantine tradition has celebrated not only the beauty of Theodora's body and the charm of her face, but also the purity of her soul, the excellence of her morals, and the power of her intelligence, in which she was superior to all the young women of her time. And, not fearing the comparison between her and the sainted mother of Constantine, the pious and holy Helena, this tradition sees in her, as a venerable biographer of saints has written, "the true receptacle of all the gifts of God."

Likewise, the Slavic traditions of the twelfth and thirteenth centuries, not content merely to vaunt her marvelous beauty, assert that she was the most distinguished, the most cultivated, the wisest, of women. Syriac traditions are even more flattering to her.

In their anxiousness to exalt the great protectress of their church, the Monophysites of the twelfth century assigned a father to Theodora, in place of the poor devil who tended the bears at the Hippodrome. He was a respectable elderly man, possibly a senator, deeply devoted to the beliefs of their sect. They added that when Justinian, drawn by the young woman's beauty and intelligence, came to ask her hand in marriage, the good papa would not give his consent to her marrying the heir to the throne except on condition that Theodora would swear never to accept the abominable canons of the Council of Chalcedon.

But the resonance of her lurid reputation had spread

as far as the remote monasteries in the West. The chronicler
Almoin de Fleury, who lived in the eleventh century, repeats
the following yarn. Justinian and Belisarius, when they were
both young and linked in the closest friendship, one day
met two sisters, Antonia and Antonina, offspring "of the race
of Amazons," who, having been taken prisoners by the
Byzantines, had been reduced to practicing the most shameful of professions in a house of ill repute. Belisarius liked
Antonina, Justinian Antonia. Antonia, who had been warned
by omens of the future of her lover, made Justinian swear
that if he were ever to become emperor, he would marry
her in an honest ceremony. Then the attachment was broken
off, but not before Justinian, as a pledge, had given Antonia
a ring.

Some years passed. The prince did become emperor.
One day at the gates of the palace, a woman of incomparable
beauty, clothed in rich garments, appeared, demanding an
audience. Brought into the presence of the sovereign, she
was at first not recognized by him, but when shown the ring,
Justinian recalled the oath he had sworn, and, reviving the
passion he had previously felt, proclaimed the beautiful
Amazon his empress without delaying longer.

The chronicler adds that the people and the senate were
somewhat taken aback by this impromptu marriage, but a
few executions silenced the critics, and Antonia shared Justinian's throne without contest.

It is easy to recognize the elements of Theodora's story
in this one. In such a narrative one gets a glimpse of how
the fabulous luck of the empress must have inspired fairy
tales in the gossip of her own time.

But whether a legend be favorable or critical, indulgent
or severe, one cannot be expected to accept it as history
unless, like this one, it retains certain essential details about
Theodora's youth. Since John, bishop of Ephesus, who knew
the empress well, refers to her somewhere—quite brutally
no doubt but also without seeming to regard it as a term of

reproach—as "Theodora who came from the bordello" (in Greek, "*ek tou porneiou*"), he confirms in general, and in a phrase, what Procopius recited at greater length.

Whatever else may be true of her, the reader must be prepared not to believe that Theodora was virtuous and chaste in her youth. Before the day she met Justinian, certainly before she became empress, she must have been a courtesan, whether obscure or celebrated matters little, and possibly even a courtesan in repentance. I am inclined to believe that, in her time, this was not a fact of vital importance, and also that, in Theodora, the empress she became caused the courtesan she might have been to be forgotten.

PART TWO

Theodora
the Empress

6
The Sacred Palace
at Constantinople

West of the Church of Saint Sophia, between the Hippodrome and the sea, on the summit and the slopes of the hill that runs down to the shore of the Marmara, rose the palace of the emperors of Byzantium in the sixth century. This was not at all like our contemporary royal residences, a more or less sumptuous edifice on some public square, following lines of symmetrical design in an imposing façade. More like the old Seraglio of the Ottoman sultans, or the Kremlin of the Muscovite czars, the palace of the Byzantine emperors included within its extensive fortified boundaries a great number of varied structures.

There were reception halls and churches, baths and hippodromes, monasteries and barracks, formal apartments of state and others for private occupancy, and elevated open terraces from which there were extensive views over the sea as far as the Asian coast. There was a whole assemblage of magnificent buildings. They were separated from each other by open courts paved with marble, by long galleries, by staircases leading up and down, and also by groves of lemon trees and handsome flower gardens that ran down almost to the edge of the sea.

This was like a separate city within the capital, colorful and mysterious, hiding in the shadows of its green trees its palaces with gilded domes, its pavilions and its summerhouses, strictly shut off from outside noises and from prying eyes without. It was a splendid and impenetrable refuge for the luxurious leisure, the elaborate ceremonies, and the complicated intrigues that filled the days of a Byzantine emperor.

Nothing could equal the richness, the elegance and the striking luxury of the Sacred Palace. Behind the heavy bronze gates that opened onto the Square of Augustus, the vestibule called the Chalké, or Bronze, which Justinian had ordered rebuilt, was a marvel of well-planned architecture and rich decoration. Under the high cupola that surmounted the rotunda, multicolored marbles and golden mosaics mingled their dazzling hues and effects. On the flooring purple porphyries, jaspers, serpentines, onyx, and mother-of-pearl were intertwined in ingenious patterns, so that the floor was as if covered with a rare carpet in which purple flowers seemed to be scattered over lush lawns. On the walls immense murals of mosaics depicted imperial victories, the generals presenting the kings and the treasures they had captured to the emperor, and among the senators arrayed in festival costume, Theodora in elaborate court dress seated beside her spouse.

Further along, past the halls of the guards, the great consistory was equally resplendent. This was the throne room, where the emperor granted formal audiences and received the ambassadors and the gifts of foreign potentates. Three doors, decorated with rich silken draperies, led into it. These were balanced by three doors of sculptured bronze on the opposite wall.

The walls shone with the sparkle of precious metals. The floor was covered with a luxurious carpet. At the end of the chamber, raised on a dais approached by three wide porphyry steps, stood the imperial throne between two figures of victory with outspread wings, from which laurel wreaths hung suspended. All of this was begemmed with precious stones and gold, under a golden canopy supported by four columns.

One side of the chamber opened out into the great triclinium, where on festival days banquets of state were served. On such occasions a sumptuous dinner service that Justinian had commissioned would be laid on purple tablecloths, including rare vases sparkling with stones and the golden dishes on which, among the bas-reliefs celebrating his victories, was carved the head of the emperor himself. Such were the splendor of the decorations, the richness of the costumes, the delicacy and variety of the fare, that barbarians who were admitted into the imperial presence or invited to the imperial table were dazzled and stupefied and, to quote a poet of the epoch, believed that, on crossing the threshold of the palace, they had entered into heaven itself.

Above the bronze vestibule were chambers. Joined to it by a series of courtyards, of galleries and wide staircases open to the sky, was another palace further up the hill, the Daphne, a two-storied structure with high outside terraces. Colossal foundations, the ruins of which excite admiration even today, countered the natural slope of the terrain and supported the luxurious edifice.

On its lower floor were installed the numerous tributary services needed for the activities of the imperial palaces. On the upper level state apartments opened onto long galleries decorated with statues. From these, entrancing prospects across gardens opened out to the sea. Further away, even more completely isolated in solitude under the shade of tall trees, were the private apartments of the sovereigns, as well as the mysterious gynaeceum, the quarters occupied solely by women and eunuchs, where the private life of the empress was concealed.

There the complicated intrigues of love and politics were spun. The emperor himself was often ignorant of what went on there, in the shadows of obscure and impenetrable cabals. After the fathers in the council of 536 had deposed Anthimus, patriarch of Constantinople, as suspected of heresy, and Justinian had threatened the excommunicated prelate with his anger, it was there that Theodora without fear offered him asylum to shield him from his persecutors. For twelve years Anthimus lived in the palace, unknown to anyone but the two chamberlains whom the empress assigned to his service. Even Justinian thought Anthimus dead or consigned to some remote exile. Stupefaction was universal when, at the empress's death, it was discovered that the saint had lived in piety, complete with his austerities and his prayers, in the tranquil and safe retreat of the imperial gynaeceum.

In addition, within the precincts of the Sacred Palace, there were countless chapels and oratories where the devoted piety of the Byzantines venerated the most celebrated saints of orthodoxy. There were still other palaces, such as that of the Magnaura, which Justinian had restored with equal magnificence. There were portals and galleries through which the private quarters were in communication, on one side with Saint Sophia, on the other with the luxurious royal gallery, the kathisma, where the court sat when attending games in the Hippodrome.

In this way the Sacred Palace, the political center of the monarchy, was closely tied to the two poles of the Byzantine world—the great church, the center of its religious life, and the circus, the tumultuous arena where the "sovereign" people expressed their wishes.

A whole community, more than ten thousand people, inhabited the city that was the palace. There were the attendants in the private imperial chambers, those attached to the personal service of the prince, cubicularies who had charge of the table, vestiaries assigned to the cloakrooms, silentiaries who imposed silence during the movement to and fro of the emperor, chartularies who recommended promotions, referendaries who received petitions, secretaries who had charge of the correspondence, a whole variegated world of officials and eunuchs—all functioning under the direction of the grand master of the household.

There was also the empress's own household, managed by the grand mistress of the palace, closely dependent on the sovereign herself, who personally distributed to her servants, women and eunuchs, the distinctive insignia of their functions.

There was the service of the imperial stables, under the master of the imperial horse, and the crowd of civilian employees who worked in all the offices of the chancery under the high authority of the master of the offices, or chancellor.

There were the soldiers of the guard, household and external, horse and foot, ceremonial troops with their handsome uniforms, their long white cloaks sparkling with golden collars, their golden clasps bearing the monogram of Christ, their gold helmets with red cockades, their lances encrusted with gold, their long splendid swords, all giving a stunning effect in formal ceremonies.

There were spathiaries, squires attendant on the emperor, excubitors, soldiers of the bodyguard, who were handsome giants who carried on their shoulders the terrifying double-bladed ax. There. were doorkeepers, heralds, bailiffs, ushers, chambermaids, ladies-in-waiting, an immense and complex crowd—and to govern all of these was the duty of the curopalatin, the mayor of the palace.

There were, finally, the religious of the church, chaplains and monks, many of whom lived in the palace quarters, and whose rough simplicity and often ragged tatters made a curious contrast with the elegance and refinement of that ceremonious and cultivated court.

The master of the offices was the chief of protocol and the supreme arbiter of the order of precedence. Under his command that whole throng, when arrayed in formal costume, was skillfully arranged in priorities of rank in order to heighten the splendor of national celebrations and the colorful variety of imperial processions.

At the New Year, the emperor, recalling ancient Roman traditions, would sometimes be pleased to revive the office of consul. Seated in the ancient chair of the curia, wearing the ceremonial Roman toga, the costume of the consuls of ancient Rome, the emperor, with a solemn and grave air, would receive the compliments of his subjects in one of the halls in the palace. He would accept the congratulations of the senate, the panegyrics of the orators, and review the long and respectful procession of the functionaries of the court.

To all he would distribute chiseled silver vases, ivory diptychs, and gold pieces heaped up in baskets at his feet, the gifts always corresponding in worth to the grade and rank of each.

Then, at the call of the heralds, the consular procession would form. It would parade through all the halls, sparkling in its accouterments and dazzling in its uniforms, as far as the Augusteum, the Square of Augustus, then to the great Church of Saint Sophia, and so on to the capitol, where, to the applause of the multitude and the rhythmic chanting of the factions, the emperor, mounted on his triumphal chariot, would drive along streets strewn with greenery and hung with scarlet banners and precious tapestries.

At other times there were formal receptions when, in the great consistory, the emperor made new appointments, announced promotions, and awarded ranks and honors. There were audiences for barbarian kings who came to do homage to Justinian, often accompanied by their wives and children, and whose strange colorful costumes excited the curiosity of the populace. There were visits of foreign ambassadors bringing gifts from their princes.

To dazzle these barbarians and to make an indelible impression on their simple minds of the vast and mighty power of Byzantium, all the refinements of luxury, all the complicated ceremonials, were brought into play. From the vestibule of the Chalké to the doors of the great consistory, the soldiers of the guard stood in line in parade formation. Under their multicolored waving standards and the sparkle of their drawn swords and upraised lances, the procession of the ambassadors would move slowly across the immensity of the splendid halls.

In the audience chamber itself, surrounded by guardsmen, eunuchs, and great nobles, seated on his throne between the two winged figures of victory holding laurel wreaths suspended over his head, was Emperor Justinian, solemn and motionless. Abruptly, at a given signal, the silken curtains over the bronze doors were drawn and the organs pealed out their tones accompanying the choirs of the factions. The ambassadors humbly prostrated themselves three times to the floor until the emperor gave them leave to rise.

Then the gifts, precious or peculiar, brought by the ambassadors, were offered to the sovereign and the interview began. It had to be in brief sentences, all regulated by protocol, formal, haughty, and stereotyped. This was followed by the state banquet, when the imperial cellar poured out its treasures before the emperor's exotic guests. Some of these had rugged faces, Avars with long curls waving like serpents; there were Huns with long hair hanging to their shoulders, enormous moustaches and tight breeches clinging to their thighs; half-naked Abyssinians wearing barbaric ornaments; dark-skinned Arabs; or lithe Iberians.

The sovereign showered them with politeness, gifts, and honors. He was especially pleased when he could signalize the conversion of some to the Christian faith and round off the reception at the palace with a baptism at Saint Sophia, where the emperor himself would stand as godfather to the newly converted.

This is how the formal life of a Byzantine ruler at the Sacred Palace, from beginning to end of his day, was minutely organized in a complicated sequence of ceremonies. In spite of this strict observance of etiquette, however, unexpected incidents would crop up that would fracture the prescribed protocol.

Maras the hermit was one of those visionary and fanatical Egyptian monks who had no respect for any human being when he felt divinely inspired. Driven from his monastic cubicle by official persecution, he betook himself to Constantinople and boldly presented himself before Justinian and Theodora. His garments alone would have been enough to cause a sensation at the palace. He wore a covering of a thousand pieces of different textures coarsely patched together with different colored threads and a cloak of the same nature, all of which was so filthy, so repulsive that, as the contemporary who recites the story tells it, even the meanest pauper would have refused it though he had nothing else to put on his body.

The language Maras used was unusually amazing. He hurled invectives at the sovereigns with such vehemence that the chronicler does not dare, out of respect for the great of the earth, to quote literally the insulting and outrageous expressions he used, so brutal and vile were they that even the lowest listener would not have tolerated them.

The crux of this incredible exploit was that Justinian and Theodora listened with exemplary patience to this man who was not impressed by the lustre of the crown or the splendor of the purple. Full of respect for this driven monk who expressed himself so freely in criticizing them, they actually declared he was a philosopher in religion. Even more, it seems that the emperor promised to consider his advice and the empress asked to keep him at the palace so she could discuss with him things of moment to God.

Zooras was another monk persecuted, as was Maras, for his creed. He too regarded it as his duty to go with some of his disciples to face the tyrant. He was well received by Justinian and invited to expound his faith before an assemblage of bishops. Instead he burst out, as was to be expected, into a tirade against the prince who persecuted the church of God, spilled the blood of the true believers, and supported the impious Council of Chalcedon. "You will have to account for all the torments to which you have subjected true Christians," he cried out, "when God calls you to the Day of Judgment."

The emperor was furious. He did not dare arrest the monk but gave voice to this threat: "It is you who are the troublemakers, the seditious ones. The council was righteous. I will not tolerate your speaking to me further in this manner. If you are right, God will manifest it to me by a sign. If not, anyone who execrates the council will be put to death."

Zooras, without fear, countered this with: "Even the angels in heaven detest your council. True believers require no sign from heaven to sustain their faith. But calm yourself. God will send you a sign meant for you alone." And he left.

The very next day, says the chronicler, Justinian went into a paroxysm. He lost his sight. He seemed hardly human. Fortunately the shrewd and wary Theodora was with him. She shut the sick man up in a secret suite in the palace, and for fear that a rumor of his death might spread through the city, she admitted no one but two doctors and two servants. Then she sent for the monk in haste. She promised him that if her husband recovered, it would immediately restore peace to the church.

When Zooras came, he observed: "Now you have the sign you asked for," and concentrating on his prayers he called the dying man back to life. When Justinian opened his eyes he recognized the old monk and realized what he had meant. From then on, full of fear of the saint, he followed his counsel in everything.

Such was life in the Sacred Palace at Constantinople about the time Theodora ruled there as its mistress. Ambitious as she was, haughty and despotic, it did not take her long to seize power with a strong hand of which she had achieved the mastery. Being, besides, all woman, always the coquette and anxious to please, she soon accustomed herself to the new sensation of majesty.

7
Theodora's Imperial Life

Rarely has a sovereign by birth loved and enjoyed more than did Theodora the manifold joys and pleasures of luxury and the innumerable satisfactions to pride that are derived from the exercise of undisputed and supreme authority. She had always taken keen delight in finery and display. At the Sacred Palace she indulged her taste for every possible elegance and refinement.

She wanted sumptuous apartments, magnificent costumes, dazzling jewels. Most of all the care of her beauty was her constant and careful study. To preserve the smoothness and charm of her face she extended her sleeping hours by interminable naps. To maintain the freshness and glamour of her complexion she took frequent baths that were followed by long hours of repose. This was due to the natural coquettishness, the desire to please, always present in a woman of her type. It was, however, also shrewd policy on her part. She was well aware that the preservation of her natural charm was the best assurance that her influence would not diminish.

Her table was maintained in the height of exquisite and fastidious taste. Justinian himself was content to live in unbelievable simplicity. He never tasted wine and ate very little. He was usually satisfied with a few vegetables. He often rose from the table without having touched any of the viands offered him. Because of his piety he often spent whole days and nights without food of any kind, so Theodora insisted that every meal she produced must include the most tempting dishes and the most varied wines.

54

She never relaxed her wish, however, to enjoy all the external trappings of power. She insisted on having her own retinue, her followers, her guardsmen, her pageantry. Being really an upstart, she adored and multiplied the complexity of ceremonial behavior around her.

The emperor made himself accessible to all. He never denied himself to anyone at his audiences. He never took exception to trifling oversights in conduct or language that might transgress the set protocol. He chatted with his visitors familiarly and encouraged them to respond naturally.

But Theodora pushed the demands of court etiquette to the extreme. From her own background in the theater she retained the taste for and appreciation of a dramatic setting. Above all, being so proud herself, she insisted that her rank be respected and that those who wished to approach her maintain their distance, perhaps secretly rejoicing to see grand gentlemen who in former days had treated her with much more familiarity now humbly bowing down over her purple boots.

For several centuries past, the ceremonial had grown very complex around the emperors, after the simplicity that had previously been preferred by the early Caesars. At the time of Justinian, especially thanks to Theodora, life at court was even further elaborated. Just as later Louis XIV did at Versailles, the sovereign wished to see great dignitaries and high functionaries busying themselves about the palace. Because the palace was the center of everything, because all important transactions were centered there, because all favors flowed from that source, it was not safe to remain absent from it, so naturally they bustled about in it.

But an extremely strict etiquette governed all relations between the courtiers and their master. Earlier it had been quite easy to approach the prince. Now they had to mold their conduct and their words according to requirements of protocol. Before, when senators presented themselves before the emperor, the patricians, placing the right hand over the heart, only had to bow deep to receive the emperor's kiss, and other members of the high assembly did no more than bow down on the right knee. No special honor was accorded the empress.

Now, however, even personages of the very highest rank had to prostrate themselves to the ground in front of Justinian and even in front of Theodora, the mouth touching the floor and the hands and feet extended, and kiss the purple boots of the sovereign. They addressed him respectfully as "Your Majesty," calling themselves his humble servants. Theodora, in particular, was extremely uncompromising on this point. She dismissed anyone who committed the slightest infraction in the ceremony as ill-mannered, to the vast amusement and open mockery of her retinue.

At that time also, the applicant was obliged to submit to a long wait in the antechamber before being presented. Theodora took special pleasure in prolonging such humiliating delays, thereby converting, as a contemporary writes, the free constitution of the state into shameful servitude.

Nevertheless, those who came were all the more eager to pay court to her. They knew her to be vain, dictatorial, and all-powerful. They knew quite well that to obtain even a slight favor elsewhere would involve them in serious peril and early disgrace. For this reason, each morning would see her antechambers crowded with applicants who were herded together like a band of slaves. The greatest gentlemen of Byzantium would be there, some having waited for several days in a row their turn to be received, raising themselves up on their toes to be seen and so attract the attention of the eunuchs who kept order.

When at last they would be admitted into the presence of the empress their gestures and their remarks were strictly regulated by the ceremonial. Never permitted to say a word to her first, they had to limit themselves to answering her questions. Generally the audience would be brief, reduced to a short and formal colloquy.

Actually, all of this, with which Procopius professes to be so shocked, was not so extraordinary in itself in a typical court life. I mention these details only to show how easily, and with what complacency, Theodora adjusted herself to the privileges of her rank. She demanded and took her share, without ever wearying, in both the ceremonies and the cares of imperial rule.

We see her receiving the symbolic golden mace from the hands of the gentleman usher and returning it as a sign of their investiture to the silentiaries attached to her service. We see her in the great consistory, seated on the throne beside the emperor, handing belted patricians the tunic and the long white veil, the embroidered scarf and the tall head-dress, the insignia of their eminent dignity. We see what was never seen before—the empress giving audience to ambassadors and barbarian kings and heaping gifts on them. We see her, winning and gracious, offering her magnificent hospitality and consideration to the rustic kings of the Iberians and the Huns. In this way, she emphasized, in the eyes of all, her sway and the influence she exercised on the general policy of the empire.

She wanted the same display and pomp everywhere she went. When she left Constantinople to take the waters for the season at Pythia, the fashionable bath in Bithynia, an elaborate pageant accompanied her, including two cabinet ministers, a crowd of patricians, four thousand soldiers, chamberlains and guardsmen, so that the movement resembled a triumphal march.

Theodora's taste for luxury was constantly making fresh demands. She persuaded Justinian to give her immense properties in Cappadocia, in Pontus, in Paphlagonia. The administration of these vast domains, from which she drew handsome revenues, required a special organization.

She loved money. She contrived to create new sources of it, even, sometimes, by most arbitrary means. She loved luxury and magnificence. She soon wearied of the Sacred

Palace, considering the ancient residence, with which so many earlier emperors had been contented, as too small and modest for her.

To please her, Justinian, at great expense, had luxurious villas built for her on the outskirts of the capital where the court then had to spend a part of each year.

Among them all the empress favored the palace of Hieria on the Asian shore of the Bosporus, an elegant country seat built on the edge of the sea, with shaded groves and running streams. The poets of the period celebrated its delights. "In this place," wrote one of them, "the Nymphs and the Hamadryads contend for rulership. One of the Graces is the umpire between them. She is unable to decide, so many most agreeable attractions are assembled here."

Another of the poets put it like this: "Sacred grove of Daphne, far from the sea, whatever may be the beauty of your rustic retreat, you must concede that I come before you. Here the Nymphs of the forest and the Nereids of the sea have fixed the place for their meeting. They contend for possession of me, but Neptune has judged that I must be divided between them."

The court was constantly being moved to this enchanting spot. The emperor came in the autumn to celebrate the grape harvest. The empress came even more frequently to seek repose and tranquility. But because, even when she only went out into the country, she had to have a numerous and attentive crowd around her, these short trips to Hieria were the despair of the imperial circle. The domestic services were ill-housed there. They often complained of the lack of the most essential facilities in the sumptuous villa.

Another ground of their dissatisfaction was that the sea crossing caused them the most terrible fear. It seems that for more than fifty years an immense marine monster had infested the Bosporus. All efforts to capture it had been without avail. It was an enormous whale, nearly fifteen yards long, that capsized ships and drowned their passengers. All the orders of the emperor to destroy it were ineffectual. The unfortunate courtiers were fearfully apprehensive when they had to cross the wide strait to get to Hieria.

At last, however, the terrifying cetacean was captured. In pursuit of a school of dolphins, the monster ran aground in the mud at the mouth of the Sangarius and was unable to extricate himself. The coastal dwellers came running when they heard the news and killed the beast with blows of an ax, then dragged it ashore and paraded it in triumph through their villages. The Bosporus regained its peace.

Moreover, Theodora never worried about the opinions of those who served her. Once she made up her mind, if it was about something concerning her own pleasure, no power on earth could make her change it. It was absolutely impossible to change her mind, for instance—however unlikely this may seem—when she decided to open her home to several intimate friends from the days of her past youth, though they were somewhat shopworn, such as the dancer Chrysomallo and the actress Indaro. She did this partly because of her strong attachment to old comrades, partly out of sheer bravado. She went so far as to allow these women a place in her councils.

Sometimes, if one can believe the *Secret History* about this, Theodora would introduce into the most serious affairs the kind of lighthearted and comic inventiveness that had made her a success as a comedian in her early days in the theater. For instance, if people came to her to complain about misdeeds of any of her close associates, she would find pleasant words with which to make light of the complaint and make it seem ridiculous in order to spare herself such annoyances. To shut off too importunate pleaders for help, she would make up the most laughable skits and act them out with extraordinary talent.

Once, an elderly patrician who had occupied high office as a magistrate owed a large sum to a member of the empress's retinue. Unable to pay his debt, he begged Theodora for an audience, hoping she would take pity on his lot. He came to her on a day when she was full of fun. She directed her eunuchs to arrange themselves around her for the reception in order to act out the comedy she had improvised for the purpose.

The old gentleman was brought into the gynaeceum. Bathed in tears, the poor chap prostrated himself at the empress's feet, as required by the protocol, and began a long speech to explain his trouble. "Majesty," he pleaded, "it is a terrible thing for a patrician to be poor. In lowly people poverty inspires compassion, but for a man of high rank such a situation occasions only insults. If a poor devil is ruined he can confess his distress to his creditors, but if a patrician cannot pay his debts he must blush to admit it. Moreover, he can never make anyone believe that a man of good birth has been reduced to poverty. If it does happen to him, he is completely dishonored by it. Now, Your Majesty, I have creditors and I have debtors. Out of regard for my position, I cannot evade my creditors; my debtors, who are not of my standing, do not hesitate to shirk their obligations to me under a thousand pretexts. So I am terribly embarrassed. I beg you to come to my aid and free me from my woes."

Theodora let him run on. Then, in a smooth voice, she began: "My dear sir." But when she got that far her eunuchs cried out in chorus: "You've got a big hernia in your behind." And each time the unhappy wretch tried to repeat his supplication, Theodora and her courtiers repeated the same response in unison. Finally the miserable suppliant, having prostrated himself as required, got up and left. It is said that the whole palace laughed heartily over the gay farce that the sovereign carried out to brush off this importunate borrower.

Such pleasantries, which do not seem too agreeable from our point of view, were not, however, frequently practiced by Theodora. If she thought about her past, she was careful not to mention it to others, and she would not willingly permit others to mention it too openly in her presence. Because she was intelligent and practical and, moreover, instinctively proud, she clothed herself carefully in her newly won majesty. For that reason, too, whatever else one may say of her, she had no intention of compromising the position she had achieved by engaging in meaningless love affairs or in frivolous flirtations.

As bold and loose as she may have been in her early life as a dancer, just so reserved, correct, careful and irreproachable did she become as the empress.

8

Gossip in a Great Capital

The great marketplace for news and gossip in Constantinople was under the arcades of the royal portico. Among the throng of idlers who gathered there every day were some who plumed themselves on bearing the title of philosopher. In the shops of the booksellers that dot that quarter, they debated all kinds of subjects—theology and medicine, politics and religion—commenting in detail on happenings at court and in the city generally.

By the grand airs they affected, their glib and high-flown speech, the deep questions with which they grappled, the ease with which they explained everything, they impressed the plebeians who listened to them with open mouths. In general they came from humble origins, without education or instruction, and usually it was the wine they had drunk that supplied their imagination and amplified their eloquence. But their audience admired them slavishly.

Men of the world saw in them only buffoons of dubious morals, eager to be hangers-on of rich houses, and, merely amused at their name-dropping and contradictions, treated them with familiarity that was often insulting and even brutal. But the mob listened thirstily to the footless discourses of these philosophers and marveled at the fine connections of which they boasted, blindly believing the tales they retailed and the news they claimed to have brought back from voyages abroad.

When Uranius, a doctor of philosophy who was very proud of the friendship shown him by the Persian king, Chosroes, casually drew from his pocket letters he had received from the great king, and when he recalled with satisfaction the intimate conversations he had had with that sovereign at Ctesiphon, the multitude said to itself that such a man must obviously be well instructed in the mysteries of politics. The more surprising the tales he told sounded, the more they met with belief among impressionable and credulous yokels.

Like every capital, Constantinople was the natural magnet for all those idlers, vagrants, beggars, and thieves whom the provinces disgorged every year. In that rabble of unemployed, restless, and discontented individuals, every bit of slander got a willing hearing, every yarn, provided it was spicy, marvelous, or strange, was picked up and hawked about from mouth to mouth.

When Anthemius of Tralles, the great architect, had thought up some new practical joke at the expense of his neighbor the lawyer Zeno, the story made the rounds of the city to the great joy of the populace. All Constantinople knew how the eminent scientist Anthemius, to play a trick on his victim, got the idea one day to set up some vessels filled with water in a basement room. Over these he installed copper pipes, the ends of which terminated between the beams of Zeno's house. After he lit a fire under the basins, the steam that came roaring up caused a kind of tremor under the house. All Constantinople roared describing Zeno's frightened face when he came rushing out into the street to ask passers-by if there were a general catastrophe that was causing great disaster.

The town was just as amused another time when Anthemius, with the aid of mirrors, deflected hot sunrays into his neighbor's house when the latter was having company and, at the same time banging some noisy objects together violently, produced what sounded like a truly theatrical storm. The public found it ludicrous in the extreme when Zeno complained to the emperor that he, an ordinary mortal, was not strong enough to battle at one and the same time against the thunder and lightning of Zeus and the shaking of the earth caused by Poseidon.

Popular superstition commented just as eagerly on all events that seemed to be omens of the future.

Constantinople had become a real museum of antiquities because of the way Constantine had gathered into it so many marvels of sculpture from pagan temples all over the empire. It was thickly populated by statues, and miraculous legends and fabulous powers were attributed to each of these.

Everyone knew, for instance, that if the great bronze bull set up near the circus were to bellow, some great misfortune would threaten the city, and that an inscription carved on a statue in the Hippodrome predicted dreadful catastrophes if only it could be deciphered. Everybody knew that a series of figures of heroes atop the columns in the forum spelled out the secrets of the future, and that Apollonius of Tyana, the learned astronomer, could read the names of future emperors from them.

Astrologers, too, were very numerous in Constantinople. Many people consulted them. Justinian was mistrustful of them because he believed they unnecessarily stirred up a populace already easily impressionable. He urged that the police treat them with all possible severity.

But the imagination and the credulity of the crowd was worked on most of all by miracles. It was an ancient custom of the churches to hand out to schoolchildren what was left over of the bread that had been consecrated for holy communion. One day a little Jewish boy was among the applicants for this bounty. His father was a fanatically religious glass blower. When he discovered that his child had eaten of the symbolic body of Christ, he shoved his child in fury into the hot kiln where he was melting a batch of glass.

For three days the child's mother, not knowing what had happened to him, searched desperately all over the city. Suddenly she heard his voice crying out to her from inside the kiln. She opened the door and found the child inside, alive and unhurt. He told her that a beautiful lady dressed in purple had carefully extinguished the burning coals around him and brought him food and drink.

The mob, delighted with such a miraculous story, added to it that, by order of the emperor, the mother and child were baptized and that the wicked father had been nailed to a cross in the Sykae outskirts.

People were just as eager to busy themselves with everything affecting the life of the court or the personality of their sovereigns. They actually knew very little but they imagined a great deal about the sovereigns' mysterious existence, of which they caught no more than a passing glimpse in the great public ceremonies. But there were many anecdotes current about the emperor. These had him alternately in close relations first with angels and then with demons.

Justinian was not one who slept long hours. Dedicated to his duties and his studies, he went to bed late, woke with the dawn, often rising in the middle of the night to resume his work. The imagination of the folk embroidered a wealth of romance about his nocturnal movements. Some said that when he wandered through the palace at night it was a headless body that roved restlessly through the empty rooms, and that all at once the head would suddenly come flying back through the air from somewhere unknown to rejoin the body from which it had been strangely separated.

Some said that servants close to the imperial presence claimed that sometimes they saw Justinian's face change its appearance horribly, his eyebrows become invisible, his eyes disappear, and every human trace vanish from it. I have already repeated the legend that has Zooras curing him by prayer of one of these frightful attacks.

Another story was that Saint Sabas, the former Palestinian ascetic, was brought one day into the presence of Justinian, fled from him like a madman, to the utter astonishment of the attendants there, and later explained that he had seen the devil in person seated on the imperial throne.

To corroborate these wonders it was adduced as irrefutable evidence that there were servants in the palace, of perfectly sound mind, who had witnessed these things and had never come back alive.

It was rumored also that the emperor's own mother had told that in a dream she had had relations with a supernatural being, with whom she had felt the contact, that it had then vanished, but that Justinian was born of this experience.

Another story was offered to explain the prodigious expenditures the emperor was making. One day, according to this account, the emperor was visiting the site of the Church of Saint Sophia while the rebuilding was in progress, heavy of heart because he was short of funds to go on and complete the project. He climbed the scaffolding and viewed the great monument with melancholy because it was destined to remain unfinished.

Just then one of the eunuchs from the palace came to him and said: "Why are you worried about money, Sire? Send me some of your high officials tomorrow. I can supply as much money as you could possibly wish for."

The next day, as the prince was again inspecting the work being done, the same attendant appeared again. "Give me some people in your confidence," he assured, "and let us go."

Justinian, astonished at this insistence, delegated Strategios the minister of the treasury, Basilides the quaestor, and Theodore Kolokynthus, a patrician who was prefect of the city, with a numerous suite and twenty-one strong pack mules to go. The eunuch led them out of the city, and suddenly before their eyes there appeared a beautiful palace that looked like nothing ever made by the hand of man.

Their guide asked the dignitaries to dismount and brought them into a great hall filled with bags of gold pieces. Then, with a spade, the mysterious leader loaded four hundred gold pieces onto each mule. That would be equal to $1,350,000 in our money. In this way he loaded the mules with about $27,000,000 and sent the deputation back to the emperor. The eunuch stayed behind to close up the hall.

When Justinian saw all the gold, he made the dignitaries describe the whole episode in detail. Because the eunuch had not returned, Justinian sent for him. But the man had disappeared, and the place where the palace had stood was empty. The emperor at once recognized that a miracle had taken place, and he attributed it to the glory of God.

The scandalmongers had other stories that they repeated more discreetly to account for the manner in which the imperial treasury was kept filled. They intimated that the emperor forged false wills to justify impounding rich inheritances, that he speculated in grain and other food-stuffs, in silks, and in the amusements of his own people, that he would not stop at any unjust scheme, even assassination, to enrich himself.

They accused Theodora and her family of similar misdemeanors. They knew she loved money and was rich. They whispered that she conspired with the emperor to strip certain of their intimates whom they had probably enabled to enrich themselves, of precious objects, beautiful textiles, and gorgeous jewels that excited Theodora's cupidity, without any color of breach of any of the laws that regulate commercial transactions.

They knew Theodora was spiteful, vindictive, and cruel, capable of doing anything to destroy an adversary and increase her own power. She was charged with the most devious and underhand plots to this end. It was said that if anyone had the bad luck to displease her, she would have them secretly ordered to the palace, and there the unfortunates, clapped into irons, blindfolded, and under heavy guard, would be put on a ship for some distant exile where ruthless jailers would implacably carry out the empress's vengeance.

The gossips of Constantinople had plenty of nourishment for their diet in all the unknown events that took place behind the impenetrable walls of the gynaeceum. Huge subterranean dungeons were thought to be concealed there, prisons in deadly silence, where Theodora had her victims locked up, beaten, and tortured. There, in perpetual darkness and confined in chains so short they could hardly sit down, her hapless adversaries were shut up for months, perhaps years, like wild beasts to whom insufficient food was thrown. If, by luck, they ever emerged from that hell, they went blind or mad or were hopelessly broken by their atrocious captivity. Any who escaped alive from this dreadful gehenna—to enter this secret labyrinth meant to abandon all hope—would be esteemed lucky. Others disappeared without leaving a trace.

Another yarn was that one day the son born to Theodora in her youth came to the palace. On his deathbed the father had disclosed his origin to the youth, who traveled to Constantinople to rejoin his mother. The empress, deeply disturbed for fear that Justinian would take it badly if he learned of this mishap in her troubled past, turned the young man over to one of her servants, one of those on whom she relied to carry out her secret plots. He was never seen again.

Certainly we must guard against swallowing all such nonsense too literally. Procopius, who maliciously gathered up all this rubbish, tells us somewhere that Theodora was a most devious woman and that if she wanted anything she did to remain hidden, no one, however clever, could penetrate her secret. It is difficult to see how any writer could have been able actually to know the truth about such terrifying stories, by their very nature extremely confidential— nocturnal assassinations, subterranean prisons, terrible and clandestine tortures.

It must be added that, even by Procopius's own admission, there were some who escaped from these infamous dungeons without too much difficulty, and more than once.

Some were among the most illustrious of the empress's victims, and some later succeeded in making notable careers.

Certainly it was true that there was ample opportunity in the Sacred Palace, so full of mysterious by-ways, for strange events to occur. The experience of the patriarch Anthimus, which I reported earlier, is an illustration of what could be hidden in the shadows in the imperial gynaeceum.

Certainly also, when Theodora hated someone, she was a woman, I believe, who would stop at nothing—neither in creating a scandal by initiating an unjust disgrace nor perhaps even in risking the outcry caused by an assassination. She was tenacious in nursing her grudges. All her life she remembered the cruelty with which the Greens had rejected her plea in early youth. She never forgave the prefect John of Cappadocia for having posed a threat to her power for a while.

To preserve her supreme authority Theodora broke down all obstacles that might block her path, frustrated all ambitions that threatened to reduce her influence. To destroy an adversary any measure was justified, even treachery or violence, mendacity or corruption. Scheming, brutal, cruel, when her own interests were in jeopardy, she had no scruples about which instrument she might choose to carry out her designs.

But, even according to the admission of Procopius himself, this implacable and violent woman was capable of pity for a defeated enemy. It is a fact that her most dangerous opponents were given no worse penalty, officially, than suffering exile for their insults or their conspiracies.

It is equally certain that this vindictive sovereign did show favor to some she had previously hated, and that, though she was of hard and despotic temperament, she remained determinedly attached to anyone who had ever served her well. It is probably a gratuitous insult to accuse her of the disappearance of her son. The daughter, who must equally have reminded Justinian of Theodora's regrettable past, did not embarrass him at all, and Theodora spared no effort to speed the success of her grandson, Athanasius, openly.

This did not stop the tongue wagging of the Constantinople gossips at all. It would have been too frustrating to their gossip and too easy to explain the profound effect Theodora had on Justinian's spirit by natural causes. It was of no consequence to these people that she was so beautiful and that her intelligence was of the first order. There certainly must have been something diabolical in the way she bent the emperor to her whims.

It was easier for the gossips to assert that Justinian was not strong-minded, that his will was as inconstant as dust blown by the wind. It was easier to allege that the empress retained her power by misdeeds, and, as nobody had any doubt that she was an instrument of Satan, it was reported that in her youth it was actually demons who fought for her favors and drove her human lovers from her chamber.

All this, to be sure, was bruited about with careful discretion. The empress was said to maintain spies everywhere. It was not safe to expose oneself to her hatred. Nevertheless, it is easy to believe that if the empress had, while on the throne, continued to the least degree the dissolute life she had lived before, any flirtations in which she indulged would have supplied ample material for the scandalmongers of the capital, who had little respect for their sovereigns in this regard.

It was generally the custom in Constantinople to cast reflections on the virtue of women, especially on those in high position, as the following anecdote will confirm.

In the Zeugma quarter, on the shore of the Golden Horn, there was a celebrated statue of Venus standing on a high column. With her protection she covered one of the most celebrated bordellos in Constantinople. She had, moreover, an additional quality even more surprising and unusual.

If a husband questioned the virtue of his wife, he would

say to her, "Come along to the statue of Venus. If you are truly chaste, the proof will be evident." Actually, only honest women were willing to risk passing by the image of the goddess because others, at the moment they approached it, found themselves suddenly stripped of all their garments by some magic spell.

From this circumstance, quite an embarrassing mischance was charged to a niece of Theodora. She was riding a horse through the neighborhood, on the way to the Blachernae palace, when a sudden downpour forced her to take a detour. Without thinking, she directed her horse to take her past the statue. Suddenly she was completely and publicly disrobed. Much irritated by this humiliation, she had the accusing statue demolished, but the jolly gossips of Constantinople were immensely diverted by the episode.

If, under these conditions, the chronicle attributes no clandestine love affairs to Theodora after her marriage; if it does not seem ever to have cast any doubt on the correctness of her private life after her marriage—it is because her conduct must have been irreproachable.

But since in later days it became almost a point of fashion to discuss her virtue, let us examine again what we must believe about Theodora's chastity.

9
Theodora's Chastity

Inasmuch as in his play Victorien Sardou has pictured a Theodora who is an amorous adventuress and libertine, one can readily agree that such an empress who, on the throne, retained the bold good looks of her youth and in spirit remained the courtesan she had been before, would hardly discipline herself to avoid her earlier habits of transgression. I would not at all wish to be so ridiculous as to sound like too resolute a champion of Theodora's virtue after her marriage.

It is, of course, well understood that it is always delicate and difficult to be absolutely certain of such private matters. Beyond that, you must believe that I do not hold, more than is necessary, to the theory that Theodora's life was beyond reproach.

I do believe that in her youth she led a pretty gay and free life, but that does not shock me in the least. If she had continued to do so later, I would feel no need whatever to be scandalized by that, and, after all, Justinian would have been the only person with a right to complain. But facts are facts. If they are examined carefully they rather prove the opposite, in favor of Theodora.

It is true that, at first impression, not one of the writers who were her contemporaries, not one historian even of later centuries—although among them there were those who bitterly attacked Theodora for her greed, her dictatorial and violent ways, the excessive influence she wielded over Justinian, and the scandal she caused by her heterodox religious beliefs—ever wrote a word that casts any doubt on the correctness of her private life after her marriage.

Procopius himself, who was so ready to slander Theodora, who piled up and recited the adventures of her youth so liberally and with such luxury of detail that we are familiar with her perfidies, her cruelties, and the infamies of her maturity, does not attribute to this so profoundly corrupt woman the slightest leaning toward any extramarital love affairs. We can agree, I think, that if the sovereign had furnished the slightest pretext for it, the pamphleteer Procopius would not have failed to recite her adulteries at length. But he has said nothing. It must be because there was nothing to be said.

But has he really said nothing? If one takes the trouble to study the text carefully, one will readily be convinced that, whatever one may have suspected, no inference can be drawn against Theodora in the Theodosius affair, in that of Peter Barsymes, or even in that of Areobindus.

Theodosius, whom we shall meet again a little later, was the recognized lover of Antonina, wife of the general Belisarius. Antonina was the empress's closest friend. Theodosius had been linked with Antonina for nearly ten years. He had followed her to Africa, to Sicily, to Italy, where she had accompanied her husband on his campaigns, without the lovelorn Belisarius ever wishing to probe into the hints he had received that would have opened his eyes.

At last, however, the deceived husband, finding he was becoming an object of ridicule, decided to take stern measures. He shut his wife up in her quarters and authorized his stepson, Photius, to take action against his mother's lover.

Without hesitation Photius tore Theodosius from the refuge he had taken in the Church of Saint John at Ephesus and had him conducted under heavy guard as his prisoner to a secluded castle in Cilicia. The operation was so expertly carried out that nobody knew what had happened to Theodosius.

It was then that Theodora intervened. It was known that she had always shown indulgence for this intrigue carried on by her favorite. Her benignity gave her a handle with which to control Antonina and, through her, Belisarius. Theodora had once before used her influence to restore Antonina's lover to her when fear of Belisarius's vengeance had temporarily separated them from each other.

This time she took even more active measures when she learned what Belisarius had decided to do. At the moment she was under a special obligation to Antonina, who, in connection with the recent disgracing of John of Cappadocia, had ably rendered signal services to Theodora.

Uneasy for her friend, the empress contrived to have Belisarius recalled to Byzantium, where she felt she could more effectively use her power to protect Antonina. She began by requiring the general to be reconciled with his wife.

But she did much more. Through spies she discovered where Theodosius was being held and had him secretly brought back to the palace. The next day she said to Antonina, "My dear, dear Lady Patrician, yesterday a priceless jewel fell into my hands, something nobody in this world has ever owned. If you would like to see it, it would delight me to show it to you." When she had thoroughly excited Antonina's curiosity, she called Theodosius out of the eunuchs' quarters, where she had hidden him.

One can imagine Antonina's surprise, her joy and her gratitude. "My savior, my benefactress, my mistress," she repeated over and over. Then, as a precaution and to shield him from the vengeance of Belisarius, the empress kept Theodosius in the palace, keeping watch that he be well treated and enjoy the best of fare. It was rumored that she even dreamed of getting him a high military command, when suddenly he died of dysentery.

That is how Procopius reports the episode in great detail. I see nothing in it to make one suppose that the empress herself stole the lover she had so diligently restored to her best friend. If the author of the *Secret History* had really suspected there was more in it than was visible on the surface, we can readily believe he would not have hesitated to hint at it in some discreet paraphrase.

Peter Barsymes was also rumored to be one of the empress's lovers. He was a Syrian who had laid the foundation of his wealth by trading in silver. He had attracted notice by the shrewdness and boldness of his questionable market operations. Later he got himself into the offices of the court prefecture. There he demonstrated such conniving ability that he pleased Theodora. She welcomed the chance to make use of him in her secret manoeuvres.

Advanced by Theodora, Barsymes won high appointment as court prefect. To account for his rapid rise the gossips of Constantinople circulated the yarn that he had certainly bewitched the empress by the use of potions and spells. He had no need to resort to such devices, however, to succeed as prefect. He was always in a position to supply cash for all the needs of his employers because of the shrewdness of his administration as minister of finance. This was enough in itself to guarantee him his position.

With a stony heart and no scruples, he ruled over his department strictly, trafficking in everything, tolerant of all exactions, speculating in grain with such immense audacity that, even before the menace of the Nika uprising, Justinian felt obliged to dismiss him from office.

But the empress's protection, though it had not been strong enough to save him, was at least serviceable enough to soften the blow of his disgrace. Shortly after his fall, this useful servitor was named minister of the treasury. There again he made himself appreciated by the skill with which he reduced expenses and organized trade monopolies lucrative to the treasury.

In the relations between this crafty administrator and his sovereign, however, there is no shadow whatsoever of amatory intrigue. Procopius says: "Theodora liked Barsymes enormously." Beyond the use by the writer of a Greek word that might signify "loving" as well as "liking," Procopius

took pains to explain the reasons for the imperial admiration
for him. "She admired him for his wickedness, for the harshness with which he handled the people, and also because he
was very skilled in the arts of magic that she herself was willing to apply."

There is no more than this in the *Secret History*. This
in itself is really no basis for making Barsymes into Theodora's lover. His success was due to other causes. The best
proof is that after the empress's death his position remained
unimpaired. Seven years after she died, he came back to
power in the court prefecture, and in spite of the hatred he
inspired in the people, Justinian stubbornly kept him in
office as a devoted and valuable servant of the crown.

As to Areobindus, he was a young barbarian, a handsome chap attached to the empress's court. Procopius says, in
brief, that Theodora was suspected of being very much
taken with him. But we must note that the author of the
Secret History, usually ready to make a positive assertion,
does not dare in this instance to take responsibility for the
story he tells. We need to study his style only a little to
recognize how much credence to give to any fact he reports
as being only in the class of "they say."

In any case, the upshot of the story is that, if indeed
Theodora felt any tenderness for Areobindus, she made it
her business to mistreat him very openly and finally to send
him away, above all, being "desirous," as the text reads, "to
absolve herself of any possible accusation." Far from attrib-
uting a weakness to her, we must in fairness rather compli-
ment her for having resisted it.

Even if Procopius literally had charged her with having
had lovers, we would still have the right legitimately to be
doubtful about his assertions. As Sardou puts it very well:
"Nothing that Procopius wrote about her has any more historical value than a revolutionary pamphlet." It is precisely
for this reason that there is something extremely significant
in the fact that the *Secret History* does not, by chapter and
verse, charge Theodora with any romantic adventure.

I do not wish to seem to draw from this circumstance any conclusion in favor of Theodora's moral qualities. She was still fairly young when she came to the throne—she was about thirty, an age at which a woman of the Orient begins to age. She was not at all young at the time she might have had Theodosius or Barsymes as a lover—she was then almost forty-five. But apart from that, she was, at the least, too intelligent and too ambitious to risk compromising the position she had been able to achieve by a love affair. Supreme power to her was worth preserving by taking every step necessary. The dignity of her station in life was perhaps of greater consequence to her practical sense than any moral consideration.

If you take the trouble to study the psychology of Theodora with some care, however, you find certain traits that incline you to believe that there was more than self-serving hypocrisy in the correctness of her conduct. For my part I am quite willing to believe that she felt some repentance and some revulsion toward her past life.

She showed herself the stern guardian of public morality, consistently demanding respect for the sacredness of the marriage tie, very little indulgent, whatever the *Secret History* may say, of extramarital love affairs. Above all she was full of concern for unfortunate girls who were more often led astray from necessity than by vicious tendencies. She occupied herself with intense zeal to save them and to free them and lift them up. We see her all her life, according to the word of a contemporary, "naturally disposed to come to the aid of women in misfortune."

Is it not perhaps because Theodora regretted not having been better protected herself in youth against the corruption of her world and the temptations of poverty? As far as I am concerned, I strongly believe that she got far less pleasure from being a courtesan than Procopius would have us believe.

Theodora was a courtesan because that was the almost inevitable consequence of being an actress, her profession, which she left fairly promptly. Rather early, religion led her to repentance. For the rest of her life she practiced serious and sincere piety. Ambition completed her entire transformation.

Once on the throne, this woman of superior mentality, of rare intelligence, of strong and resolute will, this despotic and violent creature, greedily avid of power, had other things on her mind than the pursuit of vulgar love affairs. She had some of the exceptional qualities that justify reaching for supreme authority—pride, energy, an almost masculine firmness, calm courage—all of which rose haughtily above the most untoward circumstances.

She determined to cut a figure as empress, and not solely as a would-be empress infatuated by her rise to grandeur. For twenty-one years she reigned at the side of Justinian. She governed as much as he did and probably more, a singular mixture of good and evil, of virtues and vices, of feminine emotions and the qualities of statesmanship, disquieting, complex, often disconcerting, but always infinitely fascinating.

10
The Greens and the Blues:
The Nika Uprising

In January 532 the rivalry between the circus factions had become more violent than ever, and Constantinople was in a state of turmoil.

Since her accession, Theodora, out of hatred for the Greens, had permitted the Blues license to commit the worst excesses. Justinian had reason to be extremely annoyed with this, but it always ended by his allowing his wife to have her way. If, on occasion, he would decide on some strict measure of discipline, he would soon retreat before the indignation and the reproaches of the empress.

Under her protection the Blues became accustomed to practicing all sorts of insolence. If an officer of the law displeased them, or if a magistrate had the courage to repress their excesses, the party would rise up and make an uproar to the empress against the punishment or the confiscation the officer or magistrate might order.

A count in the Orient who obtained permission to have some disorderly members of the Blues flogged was himself forced to suffer the same ignominious punishment publicly in the Antioch square.

A prefect in Cilicia had ordered the execution of two Blues who had attacked him with weapons in the streets of Anazarbus. By Theodora's orders, the prefect was crucified in the capital of his province, a victim of his determination to have the law respected.

Assassinations were being perpetrated in full daylight in Constantinople. Blues were attacking Greens with sword in hand at the very gates of the palace, practically under the emperor's nose.

If the ruler, on occasion, did not seem to respond promptly to a Blue's complaint, if he appeared disposed to protect someone with whom they thought they had reason to be displeased, they would feel no scruple against taking justice into their own hands, attacking their enemy immediately on his emerging from the imperial presence, beating him unmercifully, and sometimes leaving him for dead on the spot.

The police were powerless. They would not dare to punish the malefactors. The partisans boldly resisted even the military by armed force.

What made the gravity of the situation even worse was that the Greens, violently resenting the one-sidedness of the court, began to give a political complexion to their opposition. Many of them remained attached to the family of their former protector, the late emperor Anastasius, whose nephews Hypatius and Pompey still resided in Constantinople. Between the tyrannical and over-demanding friendship of the Blues on one side, and the ill-disguised enmity of the Greens on the other, the administration was much bedeviled. It could maintain public order only with great difficulty. With good reason it was apprehensive that some trifling incident might lead to a coalition of the factions against it.

To make matters still worse the unpopular administration of the emperor's two principal ministers—the quaestor, Tribonian, and the court prefect, John of Cappadocia— because of the excessive exactions demanded by them of the people, stirred up rising discontent. The one, though a highly educated jurisconsult, was extremely greedy and ready to do anything for money. He trafficked shamelessly in his administration of justice, violating the laws according to the wishes and the generosity of those who bribed him. The other, extremely capable but equally without conscience or scruples, stopped at nothing to wrest from subjects of the crown the money needed for the imperial expenditures. He decreed tortures, often so cruel that they resulted in death, on those he suspected of concealing their income. He permitted his agents to commit the worst depravations.

Both were universally detested by the public, but they were in great favor with the emperor, who approved their loyalty to him and esteemed them for their resourcefulness. For all these causes a persistent ferment began to rise, out of which the violent revolt known as the Nika uprising ensued. Beginning in the circus, it quickly extended over the whole city and bade fair to upset the throne itself.

On Sunday, 11 January 532, there were races scheduled as usual in the Hippodrome. The emperor was present. Without doubt, so was the empress, behind the grilles on the windows of the Church of Saint Stephen that overlooked the circus. Invisible to the crowd,. she had come to take her seat together with her retinue of lady patricians and ladies-in-waiting. The protocol in that Byzantine court, strongly influenced by Oriental customs, forbade the empress to show herself in public too frequently.

The audience was hostile. The day before, right in the city, several civilians had been assassinated. Beyond that, the Greens believed they had reason to complain of the partiality of an officer of the palace, the grand chamberlain and spathiarius Calopodius. Consequently, incessant hooting and shouts of fury rose up out of the benches occupied by the Greens. At last Justinian impatiently ordered a herald standing beside him to go over and question the critics and find out what they wanted.

The verbatim record of the astonishing dialogue that ensued between the speaker for the Greens and the emperor's messenger has been preserved. It is one of the strangest documents left to us from that period. It is also one of the most descriptive of Byzantine customs and of the liberties that were maintained by the populace in the Hippodrome, which still remembered it was the heir to the Roman people, though face to face with an all-powerful emperor.

At first respectful of the person of the emperor, the

Greens dared to name their persecutors only by obscure allusions. But soon the Greens became more heated, and they openly named Calopodius as their tormentor. They threatened anyone who would wrong them again with divine punishment. Justinian cried out with asperity: "You have come here not to see the races but to insult the government." To this the uproar from both factions increased. "Be silent," shouted the imperial herald, "you rabble of Jews, Manichaeans, Samaritans! Be silent or I will have your heads cut off!" The Greens, exasperated, shouted back: "Judas! Executioner! Murderer! It would have pleased heaven if your father Sabbatius had never seen the light of day, had never fathered such an assassin!"

Sarcasm was mixed with insults, arguments with invective. The Greens complained bitterly of being shut out of the palace and out of the government, of being deprived of all their liberties, of being constantly made the victims of corrupt authorities. "Justice only folds its arms when our faction is oppressed." And, casting in the prince's face the murders committed, to be sure, by the Blues, they cried out to him: "You let them assassinate us, and, even worse, you then order that we be punished."

Now the Blues entered into the argument, supporting the herald's demands: "Gallows birds! Blasphemers! Enemies of God! Will you never shut up?" The Greens shouted back at the herald: "If His Majesty so orders, we will keep still and respect the emperor in spite of his disregard of us. We know all about what he is doing, do you hear? But all right, we will keep still. Good night, Justice, you are dead! Good night, all of you! We are leaving. We would sooner be Jews or pagans than be Blues!"

And the Greens walked out in a body. It was the most monumental insult that could be offered the imperial majesty.

While the incensed mob left the circus and spread out through the streets, Justinian returned to the palace, confident that as usual the loyalty of the Blues would soon calm down the rage of the other faction. Unfortunately Eudemon, prefect of the city, committed a stupid blunder: in well-meant excess of zeal, he had a number of the loudest noise-makers arrested, and, without checking to see to which faction they belonged, he sentenced four to be beheaded and three more to be hanged at once. But the hangman performed his office badly for these three. Three times the rope broke under the weight of the condemned victims. Then the whole mob present demanded they should be pardoned and set them free by force. The monks in the Monastery of Saint Conon gave them asylum in a nearby church.

It turned out that one of the prisoners was a Green, but another was a Blue. Both factions united to combat this common peril. This rapidly became evident next day in the Hippodrome. Greens and Blues together insistently demanded that the emperor should pardon the offenders. The prince would hear none of it. This was a serious indiscretion on his part. Now, in the circus, instead of the former loyal greeting, "Victory to Emperor Justinian!" the clamoring mob shouted: "Long life to the Greens and the Blues, at one in showing mercy!" They rushed out into the streets with the rallying cry "Nika!" (victory), the name by which the uprising is now known to history, and stampeded through the city.

They rushed to the city prefecture and demanded of the prefect that he restore the captives to liberty. When he refused they set fire to his palace, invaded the prisons, released the prisoners, and massacred the soldiers who tried to restore order. Then all night the excited populace charged through the streets of Constantinople searching for the officials they hated so they could kill them.

The next day, 14 January, the mass of people came to batter down the gates of the palace, demanding that the chamberlain Calopodius and the prefect Eudemon be dismissed, together with the two councilors of the prince, John of Cappadocia and Tribonian. Justinian acceded to this demand: he named Basilides as quaestor and Phocas to the court prefecture. He thought the danger was allayed when he heard the acclamations and the hymns of praise the people raised when the new appointees were presented to them.

But the imperial concession came too late. It only encouraged the furious multitude by making it realize its power. The uprising turned into a revolution.

Up to that moment, however, the sensible part of the population had stood aside from these events, and all was not yet lost. Justinian believed it would be strategic to try a show of vigor. On 15 January he hurled the barbarian soldiers of the guard, under Belisarius's command, against the insurgents. Unfortunately, in the course of the fight, these rough mercenaries jostled the priests of the Church of Saint Sophia, who, to try to separate the combatants, had come out of the basilica holding the holy relics in their hands.

When the pious element of Constantinople witnessed this sacrilege it caused a general outburst of fury. A hail of tiles and stones rained down on the troops from windows, rooftops, and terraces. Women, especially excited, took a hand in the battle. Disconcerted, the soldiers retreated to the palace. To hasten their defeat, the victorious mob set fire to the public buildings in the vicinity. The senate, the Baths of Zeuxippus, and Saint Sophia became prey to the flames. The imperial palace itself was attacked. The Chalké vestibule was destroyed, together with a part of the barracks of the guard.

For three days the blaze, fanned by strong winds, spread its ravages through the city. It destroyed the Church of Saint Irene, the Xenodochium of Eubulus, the Baths of Alexander, the great Sampson Hospital (which was consumed with all its sick inmates), the shops in the marketplace, a number of elaborate palaces and private homes, and the whole quarter, one of the most beautiful in the city, that extended from the Square of Augustus to the Forum of Constantine.

More than a fourth of Constantinople was reduced to ashes. Among the heaps of blackened rubble, the remains of destroyed edifices, in clouds of smoke, in the stench of burning that made the city almost uninhabitable, through streets strewn with corpses, many of which were women, the battle went on. Pillage and burning held sway. Law-abiding citizens, facing the growing peril, fled in terror to the opposite shore of the Bosporus.

Confusion was utter in the palace. There was a shortage of guards in spite of reinforcements summoned in haste from nearby garrisons. The battalion of guards—fine handsome soldiers for a parade but not accustomed to withstanding attack—had never been more than mediocre as fighters. They were undependable except for their loyalty, and yet this time most of them, waiting to take sides until events had taken a definite turn, remained neutral between the emperor and the rioters and paralyzed the defense by their ambiguous attitude.

Justinian could depend for his defense only on some veteran regiments, newly returned from Persia, under Belisarius, and on the seasoned soldiers who formed the emperor's personal bodyguard, in all hardly two or three thousand men, and on the three thousand barbarians under Mundus who happened to be passing through Constantinople, and on the esquires and chamberlains—in short, on a modest number of the faithful dependent on his personal fortunes. These in all were few enough against a great city in uprising.

Furthermore, deeply disturbed and believing already that he saw conspirators and assassins all around him, the emperor began more and more to lose his head. At the beginning of the revolt, Hypatius and Pompey, the nephews of Anastasius, had reported at the palace to give assurance of their loyalty. In spite of their openness, the emperor ordered them to return to their homes. He never realized that by doing so he was supplying the rebels with the one weapon they lacked, that is, leaders.

On 18 January, the sixth day of the rebellion, Justinian, who had not slept at all during the night, decided to make a supreme effort. He went to the Hippodrome through the corridors that led from the palace to the imperial gallery. He had the great bronze doors of the balcony opened and appeared there holding a Bible in his hand. He promised solemnly to pardon all participants in the revolt if they would lay down their arms.

"I myself have been the cause of all this," he confessed humbly. "It was because of my sins that I refused what you asked of me at the Hippodrome." These words elicited some timid applause, but from all sides maledictions outshouted approval. "Liar! Ass! Perjurer," and stones were thrown against the imperial balcony. Insults were showered on Justinian and Theodora. There was nothing to do but retreat.

Then happened what might have been foreseen. The mob, determined to set up a new ruler, for several days had been calling out for Hypatius. They now flocked to his palace, to which Justinian had mistakenly sent him, to find this nephew of Anastasius. His wife, Marie, clung vainly to his garment in tears, crying out that they were leading him to certain death and begging his friends to come to his aid. Hypatius found it impossible to resist. The mob swept him along to the Forum of Constantine with enthusiasm, raised him up on a shield, and, in place of a crown, clapped a soldier's gold collar on his head. They brought him the symbols of empire and an imperial robe stolen during the looting of the part of the palace they had invaded.

Then, dragging along their new chief, the mob rushed into the Hippodrome and hoisted Hypatius up into the imperial box. The leaders of the riot, disregarding the counsels of moderation given by some of those with cooler heads, began to argue measures for an assault on the emperor's residence itself. At the same time the rebel party began to swell from every side, sweeping up all the dispossessed and the discontented. It took in a number of senators and nobles who came out openly in favor of Hypatius. The rumor began to spread that Justinian had taken flight with Theodora. The younger members of the Greens ran through the city with weapons, certain of their victory, and the undecided Hypatius began to have confidence in what appeared to be his destiny.

Then came the afternoon of 18 January, and a decisive moment. According to a contemporary: "The empire itself seemed to be on the verge of its demise." The city was in flames. At the Hippodrome the mob was triumphantly acclaiming Hypatius and heaping insults on the names of Justinian and Theodora. The palace seemed about to be taken over by force. Without resources and without hope, the emperor despaired of suppressing the revolt and feared he could no longer defend even his own life.

Through the gardens that ran down to the sea, the imperial treasury was hastily loaded onto ships. Justinian considered taking to flight by the same course. He held a final supreme council with those remaining loyal to him— Belisarius, Mundus, Constantiolus, Basilides, several chamberlains, and close attendants. Theodora was present at the council.

She alone maintained calmness and courage on that tragic day when Justinian, half mad, had lost his head. He saw no hope but in flight. His generals shared his weakness and succumbed to the common discouragement.

But Theodora, who had not yet spoken, suddenly rose and broke the silence. Indignant at their general cowardice, she recalled the emperor and his ministers to the duties they were ready to abandon. "If nothing else remains," she declared, "but to seek safety in flight, I do not choose to flee. Those who have worn the crown should never survive its loss. Never shall I see the day when I am not saluted as the empress. If you mean to flee, Caesar, well and good. You have the money, the ships are ready, the sea is open. As for me, I shall stay. I approve the ancient maxim that says the purple is the noblest shroud."

That day Theodora saved Justinian's throne. In that supreme conflict when his empire and his life were at stake, her ambition raised her to the stature of a heroine.

Hearing her vigorous words, Justinian and his councilors took heart and seized hold of themselves. The artful Narses, one of the empress's closest intimates, worked to detach the Blues from the rebellion by the use of cash and succeeded. Discord was set up among the insurgents by this diversion. Again some loyalist shouts of "Long live Justinian and Theodora!" were heard, and Belisarius and Mundus prepared to attack the Hippodrome.

Clambering over mounds of flaming rubble, Belisarius mounted to the imperial box where Hypatius was waiting, but the soldiers of the guard who occupied the kathisma gallery refused to obey him. They persisted in their refusal to take sides. In desperation, the general returned to the palace, believing once more that all was over, but by this time Justinian had recovered his courage. Finally, through the Chalké and the Blues portico, Belisarius, by a great effort, succeeded in cutting a passage and burst into the arena. With his sword in hand, he charged furiously into the mob of rebels.

Hearing battle being given, Mundus, who was only awaiting this signal, in turn invaded the opposite end of the Hippodrome with his barbarian troops. They forced through the entrance called the Gate of the Dead. While from the upper aisles of the amphitheater imperial troops rained a hail of arrows down on the mob, others, with sword in hand, cut wide passages through the densely packed and defenseless mob.

Then utter panic swept the circus. It was useless for any of the crowd to try to escape. The rioters were surrounded on every side. Their feeble efforts to resist were futile. The veterans of Belisarius herded them together and gave no quarter to anyone. The merciless massacre kept up until nightfall. Every individual the soldiers could reach was put to the sword. By night, when the frightful carnage ended, more than thirty thousand, some say nearly fifty thousand, corpses were strewn on the bloody ground of the Hippodrome.

Hypatius was arrested by two of the emperor's nephews. None of his supporters tried to protect him. With his cousin Pompey he was brought before Justinian. Pompey, the weaker in spirit, not made for such tragic events, wept and pleaded. Hypatius, firmer, protested his innocence, swearing that the mob had done him violence. He added that his order to the rioters to gather in the Hippodrome had no other purpose than to collect them there without defense from any measure Justinian would take in reprisal. This was actually true, but to his misfortune, his messenger had not been able to get through to the emperor to tell him so.

Nevertheless, the emperor had now recovered his self-control. He replied to the suppliants with cruel irony: "All that may be so. But since you had so much control over these people, you should have exercised it before they set fire to my capital." He had them both executed early the next morning. Their bodies were thrown into the Bosporus.

It was said that Justinian might have been disposed to forgive them, regarding the awful butchery that ended the six-day battle as punishment enough. But Theodora, more coldly cruel, demanded the executions. According to a contemporary, she swore by the holy name of God, and on her own head, never to spare the leaders of the revolt, and she had extracted a similar vow from the emperor. She called for the fulfillment of his pledge. He had to obey.

Other severities also followed. A certain number of patricians and senators, compromised during the uprising, were condemned to death or sent into exile. Their possessions were confiscated for the benefit of the treasury or distributed as rewards to intimates of the palace who had remained steadfast.

Those who seemed to have betrayed the legitimate government, courtiers who had doubted its ability to survive, soldiers of the guard who had hesitated to defend it, the members of the Blues faction who had made common cause with the Greens, were relentlessly pursued. By the emperor's orders, the prefect of the city instituted a thorough investigation, so that a new terror swept over the city.

The insurrection was subdued. Justinian was fully justified to announce in a proclamation sent to all the cities of the Byzantine Empire that he had vanquished the usurpers who had risen against him. But it was to Theodora above all that he owed his triumph. This is why the Nika uprising marks a decisive turning point in her life.

In that hour of crisis she showed herself to her imperial partner, by her coolness and her determination, to be a statesman of superior quality. She demonstrated that, on her own account, she merited a place in the council of state that before might have been accorded her only because of the weakness of the emperor. From that time forward she retained it, and the grateful Justinian did not begrudge it to her.

She had a feel for large affairs and the stamina to bring them to pass. She had a very real understanding of the necessities of government and a clear insight into what was practically possible. She governed not only as the emperor's wife, associated with him in all his imperial acts, but in her own right as a capable ruler.

Theodora's Part
in the Government

Paul the silentiary, poet, and courtier, in a piece of verse dedicated to Justinian almost fifteen years after Theodora's death and celebrating the memory of "that excellent, beautiful, and wise sovereign," recalls that during her lifetime Theodora had the active collaboration of her husband in all affairs of state.

All her contemporaries agree in saying that she had no scruples in making unlimited use of the influence he let her sway, that she exercised as much authority in government as he did and perhaps more, and that Justinian himself acknowledged this officially in a state document.

At the beginning of the great decree of 535 that reformed the administration of the monarchy and was one of the most important acts of his entire reign, Justinian was pleased to admit that, in drafting it and before making his decision to issue it, he had taken counsel with "his most highly revered spouse, with whom God had favored him."

Deeply smitten, even to the end of her days, with the woman he adored when he was younger, irresistibly submissive to her superior intelligence, her resolute and powerful will, Justinian refused Theodora nothing, neither honors nor the trappings of supreme power. During the twenty-one years of her reign she kept her hand on everything, on the departments she filled with her favorites, on the diplomatic service, on the church.

And if her influence was occasionally a cause of vexation, if her cupidity, her intemperateness, her pride, by exciting also the pride and the cupidity of the emperor, sometimes inspired measures that were regrettable, it must also be recognized that she often took a broad view of the best interests of the state and that the policies she envisioned, if time had permitted her to carry out her plans to their completion, would have made the Byzantine Empire more secure and might even have changed the course of history.

Even today most witnesses testify to the eminent place Theodora filled in the government of the monarchy. In the murals of the churches Justinian built, above the gates of the fortresses he constructed, the name of Theodora can be read together with his. In the chapels of Saint Sergius and of Saint Sophia, her initials appear alongside his. The inscriptions vaunt not only the piety that reflected glory on her name, but also the indefatigable labors and the ceaseless activity of the empress "crowned by God."

At the Church of Saint Vitalis of Ravenna Theodora's image is seen along with that of her imperial husband in the solitary apse where the golden mosaics flicker. Likewise, in the mosaic pictures that decorate the apartments in the Sacred Palace, Justinian chose to associate Theodora with his military triumphs and the most striking glories of his reign. On the imperial seals she appears beside the sovereign. All over the empire cities and provinces took pride in adopting names to do her honor, such as Theodoriad and Theodoropolis. As it did for Justinian, the gratitude of cities raised statues to her, and as they did for Justinian, those taking office swore an oath of fidelity to Theodora, who all her life was regarded as his equal.

Bishops and magistrates, generals, governors of provinces, swore "by the all-powerful God, by his only son, Jesus Christ our Lord, by the Holy Spirit, by the holy and glorious Mother of God, Mary, forever Virgin, by the four Evangelists, by the holy archangels Michael and Gabriel, to render loyal service to the most pious and most holy sovereigns Justinian and Theodora, wife of his Imperial Majesty." And in the exercise of the authority that the benevolence of the two princes had bestowed on them, "to labor without default or deceit for the advancement of their common good."

And so, as mistress over all, Theodora ruled over all in her own way, the church as well as the state. Even if at times she felt the indecisive spirit of Justinian slipping out of her grasp, even if under the pressure of circumstances or influences too strong for her to combat she would seem to give way temporarily, her bold and inflexible determination would make preparations for a future return. Scheming and ambitious, she insisted on having the last word in everything, and she usually succeeded.

By her whim, she made and unmade popes and patriarchs, ministers and generals, pursuing her own interests, equally ardent in advancing the fortunes of her friends as in cutting down the influence and the power of her adversaries. She could hate and favor with equal intensity. As high as a man's position might be, as great the services he might have rendered, as cherished as he might be by the emperor himself, just so certain would be his fall if he had the misfortune to displease Theodora. Sooner or later she would connive his disgrace. If some official flattered himself that he had risen without her protection, he could hardly have been more mistaken. Sooner or later a sudden decision would teach him that without Theodora he could not be sure of remaining on the pathway to honors.

Conversely, "the loyal empress," as she was known to her friends, never failed those to whom she had once been attached and never demanded anything of them in return but that they serve her with blind fidelity. The entire administration realized that to earn her good will was a sure guaranty against disgrace, an unfailing aid to rising higher and faster in it. They all behaved accordingly.

We have seen how she made Peter Barsymes a court prefect, and also how the eunuch Narses owed all his good fortune to her. Narses had grown up in the domestic service in the palace, a man of small stature, of slender almost frail appearance, of delicate features, of elegant manners. He early learned to appreciate the empress, her high abilities, her free intelligence, her flexible and resourceful ingenuity, her driving and cold-blooded energy. She made him her confidant, the instrument of her political designs. She made him a diplomat who had remarkable success in the confidential missions with which he was charged. She made him a general whose renown and glory offset those of Belisarius.

No doubt Theodora made some mistakes in her choices. For instance, against the advice of all she supported Sergius, who was too young and incapable, for appointment as governor general of Africa, only because he had married a relative of her closest friend, Antonina. He almost ruined the emperor's authority in his province by his stupidities. But in general those Theodora adopted showed themselves worthy of her patronage and ardently devoted to the important duties for which she recommended them.

Later we shall see that she devoted just as concentrated attention to the domain of religious affairs, defending or promoting her favorites, such as Anthimus, whom she made a patriarch of Constantinople, Vigilius, whom she made a pope, Severus of Antioch and Theodosius of Alexandria, John of Tella and Jacob Baradaeus. We shall see, too, with what fierce energy she struck at all who tried to evade her influence or tried to undermine her standing, whether they were generals like Belisarius or Boutzes, who did not submit humbly enough to her authority, or ministers like John of Cappadocia or Priscus, who dared to dispute her in spite of her power, or a pope like Silverius, who refused to bow to her will.

Against these Theodora brought into play every stratagem she had, her treachery, her cruelty, even her brutality. Thanks to the convincing lessons she gave, everybody understood that her orders must be respected everywhere, and that, if they were contrary to Justinian's, as would sometimes happen, it would be more prudent and politic to obey hers rather than his.

In short, if she wished, she would not hesitate to run counter to the wishes of her husband. One of her intimates, the Monophysite priest Julian, who lived in the retinue of Theodosius, the deposed patriarch of Alexandria, had set up a project to go out and convert the pagans in Nubia. The empress gave him strong encouragement, but when Justinian heard of the idea, he took it into his head to entrust the mission instead to orthodox priests.

He appointed a delegation charged to take a sum of money to the king of Nubia, together with precious gifts including baptismal robes. At the same time he had orders dispatched to the governor of the Thebaid that he should support the emperor's envoys by all means in his power.

What did Theodora do? She sent a short sharp letter herself to the governor of the Thebaid. This is what it contained: that her emissaries would arrive in Nubia before the emperor's, and that if the governor would not at once arrange, under any pretext he might choose, to detain the emperor's agents so that Julian could precede them, his life would answer for it. Between these conflicting but equally august instructions, the governor of the Thebaid did not hesitate. Theodora's missionaries were admitted into Nubia first, well escorted and in grand style. When those from Justinian arrived, they were given all sorts of excuses—that for the moment there was not a single beast of burden available as the empress's people had requisitioned them all—and they were shown the official orders from her, which they would not dare to disobey. When the emperor's embassy arrived it was too late. They found their places were taken, so they accomplished no result whatever. History does not say whether the governor of the Thebaid, who served Theodora so well, obtained a promotion, but we can well believe he did. It is easy to realize from a number of such incidents that they added to the prestige and the power of the empress.

It was not enough for Theodora only to fill the administration with her creatures and to see that all government employees had a high opinion of her standing. Very anxious for the best interests of the state, she had her own ideas about government policy and about appointments in the diplomatic service. There is a whole series of measures in Justinian's legislation that she certainly inspired. Some, to which we shall return presently, deal with one of her regular fields of interest, the improvement of the status of women. Others, of still greater moment, relate to reform of the public services.

With a statesman's intelligence, Theodora saw very clearly the two weaknesses that threatened the solidity of the Byzantine Empire: the financial crisis and the religious crisis.

Although she fully realized the great shortage of cash, she understood also, as did Justinian, how unwise it would be to squeeze their subjects too hard and so increase the growing discontent. It was because of this that she urged the emperor to adopt the great reform of 535 that defined the duties of all officeholders and required that from that time forward they must be equitable, honest, and paternal in the performance of their duties.

Theodora paid equal attention to questions of religion. While Justinian, fascinated with the memory of the grandeur of ancient Rome, was deluding himself with concepts as vast as they were vague and dreaming of restoring the empire of the Caesars and assuring the reign of orthodoxy by a reunion with the Roman church, Theodora, more discriminating and farseeing, turned her eyes toward the East. She sensed that the rich and flourishing provinces of Asia, Syria, and Egypt contained the real strength of the empire. She sensed the danger to the empire inherent in the religious differences by which those eastern nationalities at that moment were manifesting their separatist tendencies. She sensed the need to appease, by opportune concessions and generous toleration, the threatening discontent they were muttering. Since she strived for that goal in imperial policy, one can without paradox assert that she had a presentiment of and saw the future much more clearly than did her imperial partner.

With unremitting attention, with prodigious tenacity, with marvelous resourcefulness and ingenuity, Theodora strived until her last day to resolve the religious question, or rather the political problem that was concealed under the guise of religion. But her interest was not at all from a mere taste for intellectual controversy, from the sterile satisfaction of disputing dogma, as was Justinian's. She was of the breed of the great Byzantine emperors, who, beneath the passing and changeable forms of theological quarrels, always perceived at bottom the permanent realities of politics.

And this is why, in the best interests of the state, she went on her way resolutely protecting heretics openly, braving the wrath of the papacy courageously, drawing along the indecisive and troubled Justinian in her train, throwing herself headlong into the battle, never acknowledging she was beaten.

Until her last day she battled tenaciously for her beliefs, as a statesman, it is true, but also passionately as a true woman—pliant or brutal according to the circumstances, bold enough to have a pope arrested and deposed, subtle enough to persuade another by flattery to submit his will to hers, brave enough to protect her persecuted partisans and to supply them with the means to rebuild their church, often adroit enough to impose her policy, whatever his may have been, on the emperor.

Theodora was equally capable of conducting all affairs of the monarchy. She was ready to receive ambassadors from abroad. Those of them who appreciated her position saw to it that they paid her court. She corresponded directly with foreign potentates and they, to win her good graces, willingly flattered her upstart vanity and her unbridled lust for power. Over the head of the emperor, and outside official channels of the chancery, she carried on an entire secret diplomacy with them.

When Justinian planned to carry the war into Italy, he prepared to break off relations with Theodotus, king of the Goths at that time. The Byzantine ambassador, Peter, who was a devoted servant of Theodora, was charged with delivering the imperial ultimatum to the barbarian prince. The correspondence, mysterious enough, that Theodora carried on with the court of Ravenna at that moment seems to indicate that she had entirely other plans than those officially formed by her husband.

Must we believe, as the *Secret History* tells it, that Theodora urged the assassination of Amalasuntha, the daughter of Theodoric the Great, because she feared to find in that intelligent, distinguished, and beautiful princess a rival capable of stealing her husband's heart from her? There is nothing to prove it.

But her hand is seen in the letters in which she pretentiously proclaims her standing with Justinian in the conduct of his foreign relations. She invited Theodotus to have any requests he wished to address to the emperor delivered through her. She wrote to the foreign minister of Chosroes, the king of the Persians: "The emperor never decides anything without consulting me."

Certainly her influence was not unfailingly helpful. Sometimes neighboring courts ridiculed the empire that a woman ruled over. Beneath her statesmanlike qualities, Theodora in fact remained always all woman. For that reason she often agitated the monarchy quite unnecessarily by the violence of her feelings and the intensity of her hatreds.

She loved money. To procure it for herself she often advised measures that were oppressive and iniquitous. She loved her friends. She took care of them sometimes with an excess of solicitude for them. She assured the future of her relatives with a loyalty possibly excessively responsive to family affection.

Her older sister, Comito, the former actress, through Theodora's arrangement, married Sittas, an officer of high rank. He had been a youthful companion and remained a confidant of the emperor. She tried to marry her grandson, Athanasius, to the daughter of Belisarius to assure in this way the inheritance of the general's immense fortune. When this project miscarried, she made Athanasius, at the very least, enormously rich and very influential at court. She married her niece, Sophia, to a nephew of Justinian, the curopalatin Justin, heir presumptive to the throne. Her uncle, her mother's brother, was made a patrician and president of the senate. In the war with Persia he was given important commands. He remained one of the councilors most listened to by the emperor until the day he renounced the world and entered the monastery of Chora. Other relatives also obtained important and lucrative employment through Theodora's favor.

In short, Theodora loved power. To preserve it without having to share it, she stopped at nothing. When she felt her interests were at stake, she showed herself, without hesitation, treacherous, violent, cruel, and unforgiving to those she believed had earned her hatred. Consequently she often upset the palace and the court by the most unbelievable intrigues.

All her life she bitterly regretted not having a son who could mount the throne of Byzantium by direct inheritance from her. When Saint Sabas, the famous hermit of Palestine, came to Constantinople in 530, he was received with almost royal honors. As did Justinian, Theodora prostrated herself at the saint's feet and humbly begged his blessing. Then one day she took him aside and begged him to pray to heaven that it grant her children. Saint Sabas brusquely refused. "This woman," he explained brutally, "could bring only enemies of the church into the world." She was inconsolable that her marriage remained barren.

At any rate, as long as Theodora lived she ruled with a firm hand. Whatever her faults and her vices may have been, she made her mark profoundly on the government of Justinian. After she died, the decadence that set in, under a prince aging and weary, made Justinian's reign, which had been so long and so glorious, end in sadness and in gloom.

12
The Hatreds Theodora Bore

Among the princes in the imperial family, Justinian's nephew Germanus, a patrician, was the most unusual and the most popular. An admirable soldier, an energetic general, an able diplomat, he made a success of every task with which the emperor, whose confidence he enjoyed, charged him. He had distinguished himself especially in Africa where, by a skillful combination of opportune concessions and strict firmness, he had been able to subdue a dangerous insurrection and restore peace and order to the province in a few months.

Wherever Germanus went he left the finest impression. The army adored him. From the time he was appointed commander-in-chief, the mercenaries eagerly enrolled under his banner. Even the barbarians felt honored to serve under his orders. The subjects in the provinces admired him for his courage, for the fairness with which he conducted his administration and dispensed justice, and for the terror his name alone inspired in the enemies of the monarchy.

He was appreciated just as highly in Constantinople. He conducted himself at the palace and in public with calm and proud dignity, much concerned about preserving the government's good name and observing the laws scrupulously. He kept himself carefully free of the intrigues that too frequently agitated Justinian's court and, what was rare in Constantinople, he never shared in the partisan feelings that ran high at the circus or in the rivalries between the factions.

Very rich, Germanus was generous with help to all

those who asked it of him and never asked for payment of interest. In short, with his friendly and amiable disposition, he did not deem it necessary to display arrogance in his princely rank. He entertained well and was most obliging in hospitality both in his drawing rooms and at his table. For these great qualities, these rare virtues, Germanus was one of the noblest personalities in Justinian's circle.

But for the same reasons he was out of favor at court. Too well liked, too popular, he rather disquieted the mind of the emperor that was ever suspicious. Too steady, too distinguished, too generous, he displeased the empress even more because his conduct seemed too obvious a criticism of the bearing usual among sovereigns. Besides, Theodora detested him as a possible heir to that empire that she so longingly hoped to assure to her own posterity.

Possibly she also took it amiss that Germanus had made too brilliant a marriage by wedding the granddaughter of Theodoric the Great, which only underscored rather too emphatically the humble origins of the empress herself. But above all she sensed in him a potential rival, whose high standing she must at all costs cut down. She was not sparing of the points of disfavor she held against him.

Little by little, under the influence of his wife, Justinian, who earlier had been quite willing to make use of his nephew's talents, ended by keeping him at arm's length, almost in disgrace, without calling on him for any service. At the same time he let Germanus's two sons, whose ambitious and eager nature also aroused his suspicions, languish in most obscure appointments. Each day the marks of the emperor's disfavor became more apparent.

Germanus's brother, Boraides, died, bequeathing the largest part of an enormous fortune to Germanus and his sons. Justinian immediately annulled the will under the pretext that the decedent had left a wife and daughter, whom he had no right to disinherit in this manner.

Theodora's hatred showed itself so openly that other

families feared to ally themselves with that of Germanus. Besides his two sons Germanus had a daughter who, at eighteen, had not yet married. Soon a suitor presented himself. He was John, a nephew of Vitalian, who had once tried to outweigh the influence of Justinian at Justin's court. Though John, because of his parentage, was regarded with disfavor at the palace, he was brave, courageous, and immeasurably ambitious. He believed that, as he could expect little from the government side, he might as well seek his fortune from the opposition and so asked Germanus for his daughter's hand.

It was a poor match for the grandniece of an emperor, but Germanus welcomed this unexpected son-in-law enthusiastically. The two men, each for his own reason having considerable fear that this cherished project might be frustrated, bound themselves to each other by the most solemn oaths.

At news of this, Theodora flew into a violent rage. She tried to prevent the marriage by every possible means, by intrigue and by threats. Nothing she could do would stop it. She ended by declaring openly that John would pay for his daring with his head. Because, apart from this, the young officer had been involved in a misunderstanding with Belisarius, it was with much apprehension that John rejoined the forces in Italy as soon as the marriage was celebrated.

There Antonina, Theodora's most intimate friend, met John, the soul condemned by Theodora. Nobody doubted that the empress would charge that skillful conniver, Antonina, with the carrying out of her vengeance. To Theodora's credit, however, it must be added that the son-in-law of Germanus does not seem to have had to repent of having dared to brave the sovereign's animosity.

Germanus and his sons were less fortunate. As long as Theodora lived, they remained in disgrace. By the slanders she concocted against them, she succeeded in poisoning Justinian against them so thoroughly that even after the death of his wife it was a long time before the emperor would believe they were loyal and reopen the pathway to honors for them.

In this way, to maintain her hold over Justinian, Theodora took pains to shunt aside all those whose influence might counterbalance hers. Her hostility was even more pitiless for any who dared to dispute her authority or tried to reduce her standing.

In 542 Justinian fell seriously ill of the plague that was then ravaging Constantinople. Rumors of his death were already spreading through the capital and the army. Several of the generals, hoping to benefit from a change of regime, declared that in case he were to die they would not leave it to Byzantium alone, meaning the palace and the empress, to set up a successor as emperor.

To Theodora this was an unforgivable presumption. As soon as the emperor's recovery reaffirmed her complete authority, she ordered the chief culprits, Belisarius and Boutzes, who had been denounced to her by her spies, to report to Constantinople. Belisarius was abruptly relieved of his command. He fell into complete disgrace and for a time even feared for his life.

Boutzes was invited by Theodora to report to her in the gynaeceum to receive an important communication. There he was arrested and confined in one of the subterranean dungeons where it was said the empress's victims disappeared. For over two years he languished in that hell, living in perpetual darkness, not speaking with a living soul. The jailers who brought his food were ordered never to exchange a single word with him. Everyone outside thought he was dead. Out of caution nobody dared even to pronounce a name that brought up such sinister recollections.

Suddenly one day Boutzes reappeared. Theodora had finally taken pity on her victim, but in restoring him to liberty she sent him out practically unrecognizable. According to Procopius, Boutzes was left almost blind by his long captivity, and his health was irretrievably ruined.

A similar disgrace struck down the secretary Priscus. By Justinian's favor he held the high position of commander of the guards, where, proud of the marked interest the emperor had shown in him, he thought he was of a high enough standing to combat Theodora. Essentially evil, his duties gave him intimate knowledge of all affairs of the emperor, whom he pleased by an affectation of zeal and devotion.

First of all, he took advantage of his position to accumulate a considerable personal fortune. But he dreamed of going much further. Relying rather imprudently on the emperor's friendship, and inflated by the important connection to which he had been raised and the responsibilities with which he had been entrusted, he put on arrogant airs and an attitude the empress found disrespectful. He went so far as to speak of her in terms she deemed highly insulting.

Theodora was never a woman to tolerate such familiarities, but Priscus's influence on his master was so strong and the emperor's affection for his councilor was so real, that at first she could get nowhere. So she decided she must take bold and vigorous action. She had her enemy Priscus conveyed to Cyzicus by force. There he was promptly tonsured and inducted into holy orders. After the accomplished fact, Justinian gave in with his customary weakness. He never even asked what had happened to Priscus. He was satisfied with confiscating the immense fortune his former favorite had acquired and keeping it.

Many other people were also made to feel the implacable violence of Theodora's hatred. Bassianus, like Priscus, presumed to act impertinently toward the empress. This was taking a great risk, especially since he had the misfortune to belong to the Greens. Bassianus, realizing the danger he was exposed to, sought asylum in the Church of Saint Michael Archangel. Without respect for the sanctity of the

church, Theodora had him arrested there, but she was too
clever to let it seem this was only because of an insult to
herself. He was imprisoned on a charge of a breach of sex
morals and promptly sentenced by a cooperative magistrate
to the capital punishment prescribed for such a crime. The
multitude, moved by the grace and beauty of this elegant
young man, cried out in vain for his release, but, by a refinement of cruelty, Theodora decreed that a shameful mutila-
tion be added to the usual penalty of death. Then, in
accordance with her practice, she had the victim's fortune
confiscated for the benefit of the treasury.

She was just as ready to take revenge for affronts to her
friends or theirs. When Photius, Belisarius's stepson, agreed
to defend his stepfather's family honor and dared to carry
off Antonina's lover in open daylight from the church at
Ephesus, Theodora made him pay dearly for that audacious
piece of violence. She had him arrested and flogged like an
ordinary slave. Then he was subjected to the most atrocious
torture to force from him the secret of the place where he
had hidden his prisoner. But unexpectedly that man of delicate health, that elegant man so careful of his own body,
showed unprecedented resistance under torture. Then Theodora had him locked up in one of her terrible underground
dungeons.

Photius managed to escape and went for asylum into
the Church of the Holy Mother of God. He was recaptured
and imprisoned again. Again he escaped and this time took
refuge in the Church of Saint Sophia itself, confident that
no one would dare to tear him away from the altar venerated by all. But nothing could appease Theodora's hatred.
By her orders, the clergy of the great church, overcome with
fear, delivered up the refugee. For the third time Photius
was imprisoned. There he sat for three years. He was beginning to despair, when, as it was said, a miracle came to his
rescue.

The prophet Zacharias came to him in a dream and
promised to help him take flight. Once more Photius suc-

ceeded in escaping from the imperial prisons. This time, more fortunate, he got as far as Jerusalem after outwitting the agents dispatched to pursue him. There he entered a monastery, believing it would be the only way to elude Theodora's vengeance. Much later, after Justinian's death, he was to return to the palace and to become, strangely enough, the favorite of Empress Sophia, the very niece of his former persecutor.

All those who had aided Photius shared in his disgrace. Several of his intimates were either flogged or exiled by Theodora's orders. Others disappeared mysteriously. His friend the senator Theodosius, who had taken part in the exploit at Ephesus, was subjected to an especial atrocity. He was thrown into the empress's underground prisons and chained up like an animal in fetters so short that it was impossible for him to sit down. He lived there, obliged to remain constantly standing, eating and sleeping like a beast. After four months of this treatment, he went violently insane. Then he was released, but he died a short time later. His possessions were, naturally, confiscated.

Sometimes Theodora's vengeance, however, would misfire. Diogenes, a man of noble birth, was extremely popular in the capital. The emperor liked him immensely even though he belonged to the Greens. Just for that reason the empress detested him and set herself to destroying him.

Procopius neglects to explain why, under such circumstances, Theodora chose to resort to other than those secret and mysterious measures she usually adopted. She had Diogenes indicted under moral charges and sent before a court for a public trial. She took pains beforehand to suborn witnesses from among his own slaves to testify against him. But the judges, taking their role seriously, did not regard the depositions submitted as sufficiently convincing.

To strengthen the prosecution, Theodora had one of the defendant's servants arrested, and by alternating flattery and violence she tried to persuade him to testify against his master. But she got nowhere by these means, so she had a cord tied around his head and tightened until his eyes were bulging from their sockets. In spite of everything the man would not give in. At last the tribunal, deciding the case was clear, acquitted Diogenes to the applause of Constantinople and the great discomfiture of Theodora.

If you wish to examine some of these anecdotes that I have taken from the pages of the *Secret History* more closely, you will, I have no doubt, find more than one detail to be viewed with caution. It must be admitted that it is difficult to understand why, when she had so many devious but sure ways of destroying her adversaries, Theodora sometimes took pleasure in sending them to a public trial and running the risk of their being acquitted.

On the other hand it seems clear also that some prisoners could escape easily enough from those forbidding underground prisons of which Procopius gives such a somber and dramatic picture. The case of Photius proves that. And the example of Boutzes himself, who, after having passed through them, reappeared not only in the councils of the emperor but at the head of the armies, shows that a prisoner who emerged from them was not necessarily reduced to the state of a living corpse such as Procopius chose to represent the unfortunate general Boutzes.

In short, Procopius's own admissions that the terrible Theodora was sometimes capable of pity and pardon do not exactly accord with the implacable hatred he ascribes to her. It is also a fact that some of her most dangerous opponents paid the penalty she exacted for their opposition to her only by exile and not by death, which to some extent contradicts the sanguinary inclination Procopius attributes to her.

But without unduly extending the catalogue of her cruelties and her victims, it is still not necessary to make her out too merciful or forgiving. When her interests were affected, she stopped at nothing. Even an assassination would not deter her if she considered it necessary or useful.

The experience of Priscus or that of Germanus show to

what lengths Theodora went if her power were questioned. The story of the disgrace of John of Cappadocia is even more characteristic. It throws light on the customs of that Byzantine court. At the same time it illuminates more clearly the vehement character, the ambitious soul, the vindictive spirit, the unscrupulous energy, the ingenuity in perfidy, of Empress Theodora.

13
Theodora and John of Cappadocia

For ten years John of Cappadocia served in the eminent capacity of prefect of the court. This made him at the same time the minister of finance, the minister of the interior, and practically the prime minister of the monarchy. Rising from the very lowest and humblest origins, with little breeding and only a negligible education, he gradually insinuated himself into the favor and friendship of Justinian by his superior intelligence, the shrewdness of his powerful and practical genius, and his marvelous comprehension of business.

John of Cappadocia had attracted the attention of this ruler, who was always short of cash, by fulfilling glittering promises and completing grandiose projects for the financial reorganization of the treasury. Soon he was promoted to higher posts in the administration and not long after to even more illustrious dignities, so that by 531 he had reached the elevation of prefect of the court.

A proverb of that era says: "The Cappadocian has an evil nature. Give him a position, he gets worse. Show him how he can make some money, he becomes more detestable than ever."

By his toughness, his avarice, his freedom from scruple, the prefect amply justified the undesirable reputation of his compatriots. To find sources of cash, either for himself or for the treasury, he sacrificed human lives and ruined cities, coldly, pitilessly, and remorselessly. He allowed his agents to do anything they chose, provided they gathered the gold, and he himself set the example for them by showing them how to get it.

He installed a whole equipment of scientifically designed instruments of torture in the prefecture prisons. Those whom he suspected of concealing their fortunes learned there what it would cost them to try to defraud the treasury. Beaten, suspended by their hands or their feet, tormented by a hundred devices, often so that death would result, people of every station and every age were subjected to his cruelties. At his hands, according to the word of a contemporary, his victims only emerged either plucked clean or dead.

With his vulgar and avaricious nature, John of Cappadocia, though he worked for his emperor, never forgot to take care of himself as well. A writer of the period said of him: "Always ready to steal, he speculated in everything. When the army took ship for the reconquest of Africa, the prefect, on whom it was incumbent to furnish all the supplies, delivered breadstuffs of such poor quality to the troops that it could have caused an epidemic in the expeditionary forces on their way, but John of Cappadocia made a great profit from the operation."

He speculated in grain, either requiring the producers to pay in gold the taxes usually payable in kind, or buying up the entire harvest so that he could resell the crop at famine prices. He took discounts off the pay and the pensions, pocketing the difference. By all these devices and impositions he built himself an immense and scandalous fortune.

Everybody hated John of Cappadocia. But he had one great merit in Justinian's eyes. He supplied the money for every demand to meet the enormous disbursements of the regime. Whatever means he resorted to for this admirable result, the emperor was not too concerned about and even preferred to ignore them. In any case, by the ingenuity and constant care he displayed in finding sources to increase the public revenue, for which the emperor praised him publicly, and for still other services he rendered, the prefect made himself indispensable to the emperor, who forgave him everything else he did.

In spite of the hatred he aroused, everyone at court, trembling with fear of the all-powerful favorite and in order to please the emperor, endlessly praised John of Cappadocia's impressive ability and the success of his administration.

His oppressions were a large contributing factor to the outbreak of the Nika uprising, and this riot arrested the growth of his fortune for a while. He was in disgrace, to the great and enthusiastic applause of all Constantinople. But he was the indispensable man. Before long he returned to power, more avaricious than ever, and just as assured of his master's favor. After all, he was the court prefect, he was a consul, he was a patrician. Justinian, in an official decree, thanked him "for having the emperor's well-being so deeply at heart," and ended by entrusting himself blindly to this useful and devoted servitor.

All-powerful over the emperor's thinking, and also by this time prodigiously rich, John gradually became intoxicated with his good fortune. With his essentially vulgar nature, sybaritic and sensuous, he loved power for the material pleasures it could provide. He loved good living, good wines, delicious dishes. He would appoint a cook to high public office if the cook served a particularly successful meal. For his table he sent to the Black Sea and to even more remote shores for the rarest fish and the most expensive wildfowl. A big eater and a heavy drinker, he passed entire nights feasting with jolly companions, not permitting himself to be disturbed even for affairs of state. It was not unusual to find him of a morning completely drunk or so gorged with food that he would cover the floor around him with his vomit.

His manners were deplorable. He would be seen passing through the streets of the capital dressed in a green costume that made the pallor of his complexion stand out and surrounded by a scandalous procession of gay young people and courtesans. Clothed in transparent garments that showed off their beauty very clearly, this swarm of light women surrounded the powerful minister's litter, covering him with kisses and caresses, while John, nonchalantly lounging on the shoulders of his favorites, reckoned by this picturesque and careless display and this grand show of luxury, that he would dazzle the eyes of his fellow citizens and prepare them for the future of which his ambition dreamed.

Like most people of his time, John was exceedingly superstitious. He believed in omens and in fortunetellers. These seers happily foretold to him that one day he would wear the robe of Augustus. To aid the realization of these predictions, John resorted to magic incantations. All puffed up with his hopes, he saw himself already as emperor and seemed, according to the pretty expression of Procopius, "to be walking on clouds."

John of Cappadocia believed in neither God nor Satan and was strongly suspected of being addicted to paganism. In that devout orthodox court, he had the daring to appear only seldom in church, and then, instead of Christian prayers, he muttered pagan litanies under his breath.

At home it pleased him to revive the ceremonials of ancient Greece. Robing himself like a high priest, he prayed to dogs and demons, hardly being able to distinguish between them, to maintain his influence over Justinian while awaiting the hour when he would overthrow the emperor. Meanwhile, as he had a practical sense as well, he made use of his immense fortune to build up a following in the empire. He made it a practice to go on tours through the provinces, in grand style, to make himself well-known in them.

To prepare the way for himself John had no fear of entering into conflict with Theodora. Instead of flattering her and paying her the respect she expected, he began to assume a haughty and insolent air toward her. He openly criticized her to the emperor, hoping to turn into dislike the great affection that Justinian bore for his wife.

These were things Theodora would never forgive. From then on the battle was joined, relentless, inexorable, between the minister and the sovereign. She, ready for anything, only awaited an opportune moment to ruin her rival. He, realizing well that Theodora was the greatest obstacle in the path of his ambition, spared no effort to block her.

In this bitter but undercover battle, John of Cappadocia was aware of what a redoubtable opponent he was attacking. He knew Theodora was capable of anything, even of getting rid of an enemy by assassination. So, at night, in spite of the thousands of guards with whom he surrounded himself, sinister thoughts often troubled his repose. Starting up at every sound, he would think he saw some barbarian mercenary hired to cut his throat springing up at his bedside and, uneasily straining his ears, John would try his doors, peer into dark corners, and then be unable to close his eyes in sleep again.

But by day he would regain his courage. He was well aware of the imperative need Justinian had of his services, of the prodigious domination he exercised over the emperor's mind. He relied also on the inextricable disorder that, by design, he had introduced into the conduct of the treasury, which made him indispensable because no successor would be able to unravel it.

But it was under the eternal watchfulness of Nemesis, who, as a contemporary wrote, always repays evil for evil, that John pursued the course of his exactions and his crimes, enriching himself and his friends, filling up the administration with his intimate friends, continually increasing his scandalous fortune. Everybody bowed in respect for his all-powerful influence, though the chroniclers spoke of him as "the enemy of the laws," or "the basest of all men," and nobody in the palace dared to mention his name without showering praises on it.

John of Cappadocia failed, however, to take into account the depth of Theodora's intrigue. First she tried to enlighten Justinian on the sufferings the prefect's administration inflicted on his subjects, on the rising discontent they were stirring up, on the peril with which they were threatening the monarchy itself.

Very slyly, the empress set to one side her personal grievances, and appealed only to the emperor's political good sense, to the intense liking he was known to have for order and exactitude, to the solicitude that moved him for the happiness of his people. She got nowhere. Justinian could not bring himself to deprive himself of a minister who even his enemies admitted was "the ablest genius of his time" and so marvelously expert "to foresee all eventualities and resolve all difficulties."

Then Theodora tried to arouse the emperor's suspicions at the danger the prefect's ambition presented to the authority and even to the life of the sovereign. Justinian would hear none of it, in spite of the readiness with which he usually received slanderous communications and with which he would give up even his best friends when impressed by the slightest move that would arouse his jealousy.

Like all other weak characters, he hesitated to dismiss a counselor to whom long habit and a real sense of affection seemed to have attached him deeply.

Theodora began to feel considerable embarrassment. She could not risk a show of force against the all-powerful minister to overcome the emperor's obstinacy, as she had done with Priscus. John was too carefully guarded to let her hope to get rid of him by poison or by poignard. But she was resourceful. She devised a diabolical scheme to destroy him.

Antonina, the wife of Belisarius, had then just come back to Constantinople from Italy. Grand mistress of the palace and utterly devoted to the empress, this bold intelligent woman, an excellent conniver whose feelings ran strong, had no equal—as Procopius, who knew her well, wrote—for plotting an intrigue and succeeding at the impossible. In several situations she had already shown the measure of her skill and rendered signal services to the empress. At that moment she was especially willing to do the sovereign a good turn because Theodora knew all her secrets and covered up her amours for her. Antonina was therefore entirely receptive to Theodora's design. She detested the prefect in any case.

She knew how the renown of Belisarius eclipsed that of John of Cappadocia, how jealous the minister was of the prestige and popularity of the general. However dubious was Antonina's fidelity to her husband, she was careful to protect him from any public disgrace to which she might be a party. Therefore she lent herself willingly to Theodora's proposals, and to please her she applied all her zeal to the sinister intrigue that the two women together plotted out.

John had a daughter, Euphemia, who was still quite young, frank and naive, and his only child. She was his pride and joy. Antonina made up to her. By daily visits and flattering phrases, she insinuated herself into friendship with her. Making a confidante of her, Antonina opened her heart to Euphemia. One day when they were chatting as usual, woman to woman, Antonina began to speak about the dissatisfaction Belisarius felt. She complained bitterly that after having conquered Africa and Italy and bringing back two captive kings and uncounted treasure to Byzantium, the victorious general encountered nothing but ingratitude from his imperial master. She took this as a text for severely criticizing the form of the government. Euphemia trustingly listened to these dangerous sentiments, and as she, too, distrusted and detested the empress, in whom she saw only her father's enemy, she asked very ingenuously: "But my dear friend, why do you have to tolerate such indignities, when you have the army in your hand?"

This was just what Antonina was waiting for. "A revolution only in the army camp," she explained, "is quite impossible without a firm ally in the capital. If only your father were willing to be that ally, we would not find it difficult to succeed, with the aid of God."

This conversation was naturally reported to the prefect by his daughter. He was enchanted by the idea, thinking that already he could see the oracles that had promised him the throne being realized. He sent word to Antonina that he would be happy to talk it over with her next day. To put the minister off the track and to avoid all suspicion of treason on her side, the wife of Belisarius refused to take part in such an interview. It was, she pointed out, too perilous a game. In a capital filled with spies and informers, there was great risk of being trapped and so losing everything. But, she added, she had to rejoin her husband in a few days at the army of the East. She could, she suggested, stop on the way at a remote villa that Belisarius owned in an outskirts of Chalcedon on the Asian side. Under the pretext of paying her a call, the prefect could go there without much effort. There it would be possible to talk freely and discuss setting up an alliance.

The display of so much caution pleased John of Cappadocia. He set a day for the interview. Meanwhile, Theodora, who was kept informed by her favorite of the progress of the affair, likewise passed this information along to Justinian. The emperor persisted, however, in his refusal to credit it. He could not bring himself to believe that the minister would conspire against him.

With some difficulty the empress persuaded him to send two of his loyal officers, the eunuch Narses and the commandant of the guards Marcellus, to the decisive meeting at the villa. Concealed there with the help of Antonina, they were to burst in on the interview. If they were certain it was treason, they were to arrest the prefect, and, if he resisted, put him to death at once. Theodora was hopeful that in this way her enemy would be disposed of in the hubbub, without being given time to explain or to justify his presence.

At the same time that he agreed to indulge the empress's wish, Justinian, as a last act of affection, took it in hand to warn his favorite not to show himself at the fateful house. John of Cappadocia took no notice of this advice. He crossed the Bosporus at night, as had been agreed, and, cloaked in mystery, he went on to the villa. He did take the precaution of taking along a companion.

John was received by Antonina in the garden of the villa. He promised to do everything she asked. He solemnly swore to work for the emperor's downfall. At that moment, Narses and Marcellus, who had heard all this while hidden behind a hedge, suddenly leapt forward from the shadows and tried to arrest the minister. At the noise, John's guards came running. There was a fight. Marcellus himself was wounded in the affray and finally the prefect got away. Regaining the capital in haste, he fled to take refuge in the inviolable asylum of Saint Sophia.

This is what defeated this clever man, who usually kept a cool head and more presence of mind. If he had dared to present himself boldly to the emperor, he might have succeeded in convincing the sovereign of his innocence. By fleeing, he acknowledged his guilt and, moreover, he left the field clear for Theodora. She demanded his immediate dismissal by Justinian. According to Byzantine usage in such instances the minister was compelled to take holy orders at once. Without delay, right in the Church of Saint Sophia, and in spite of his resistance, John of Cappadocia was tonsured. As there was no free and available monastic habit on hand at the moment, to get it over with quickly, they threw over his shoulders the habit of a monk attached to the treasury of the basilica who happened to be standing by.

Procopius reports that the name of this monk was Augustus, so that the oracle had not lied in predicting that one day John would wear the robe of Augustus.

John of Cappadocia never resigned himself to his new status. He never consented to perform his duties as a priest.

He never meant to close the road for his return to public office. Trusting to his luck, he kept up his hopes and flattered himself that he would soon return to favor. Actually, Justinian treated him with extreme clemency. Exiled to the neighborhood of Cyzicus, John was able to reclaim a large part of his confiscated assets through the mercy of the emperor. As he had shrewdly enough, during the days of his prosperity, transferred a considerable part of his fortune to safe hands, he remained very rich. In his peaceful and luxurious retreat, he lived handsomely, truly happy except that he could not console himself for the greatness he had lost.

Public opinion in Constantinople was righteously indignant that so vicious a man expiated his crimes so lightly, and, contrary to all justice, lived an existence more agreeable than ever before.

Fortunately for morality, Theodora kept watch. In this dangerous crisis, the most serious she had lived through since she became empress, she had, for a moment, feared for her power. She never forgave this man who had threatened her standing. Her hatred for him, still unappeased, was never allayed. Her vengeance did not spare any effort to destroy her rival. She followed him until her dying day.

The head of the church in Cyzicus was Bishop Eusebius, a man universally detested. His dismissal had been demanded of the emperor but in vain. By his intrigues and his influence at court, he had always held his position. Finally, discontent rose to such a height that a conspiracy against him was formed. He was assassinated in broad daylight in the forum.

Now it was known that John of Cappadocia had been on bad terms with the bishop. Theodora eagerly seized this opportunity to get him involved in this affair. A senatorial commission was sent out to open an inquest. John was arrested, imprisoned, and flogged like an ordinary thief or highwayman. His innocence was so obvious, however, that it was impossible to sentence him to death. At least, to please the empress, he was despoiled of all his possessions, down to the clothes he was wearing. They left him only one wretched tunic, and he was put aboard a ship to Egypt. To complete the humiliation of this former minister, the captain of the ship was ordered to put John ashore at every port of call and make him beg for his bread from passers-by. This former prefect of the court, this former patrician, this former consul, denuded of everything, was seen having to hold his hand out for food to live.

Finally, he was sent to Antinoe. Even there Theodora's vengeance pursued him. She traced the assassins of the bishop of Cyzicus and, by promises and threats, got one of them to accuse John of having actually plotted the murder. But the other, in spite of tortures, refused to lie and save himself by accusing an innocent man. John escaped as well, but until Theodora's death he lived in exile, miserable and often mistreated by his jailers.

Nevertheless, even in his misery, this energetic man never lost his courage, his self-confidence, and his insolence. This prisoner of the state, remembering that he had once been minister of finance, amused himself by reminding citizens of Alexandria that they still owed sums in arrears to the treasury.

This exile, poor and abandoned by all, still dreamed of the empire he had hoped to rule. The very day after Theodora's death, he returned to Constantinople, audacious and bold as ever, having never lost faith in his star. But he was too late. In seven years Justinian had forgotten his former favorite, and John of Cappadocia was unable to climb back into favor. He died in the monastic robe in which, against his will, he had been clothed.

Theodora found an adversary truly worthy of her in this all-powerful minister, who was as intelligent, ambitious, and unscrupulous as herself. Against him she exhausted all the resources of her fertile imagination in schemes attributed to her by the chroniclers. She could legitimately take pride in her victory over him in the relentless struggle in which she engaged.

It was by other means, just as ingenious, that she was able to hold the adherence and fidelity of another man whose influence she thought she had equal reason to combat. The story of her relation to Belisarius and to his wife, Antonina, is equally as instructive as that of her struggle against John of Cappadocia for a thorough understanding of her character.

14
Theodora and Belisarius

By the brilliance of his victories, by his prestige, his wealth, and his popularity, Belisarius could well seem to Theodora to be her rival for influence, like John of Cappadocia and possibly even more dangerous, because Belisarius held in his hand that force, the army, which in the Byzantine Empire was the essential instrument for any successful revolution.

Belisarius was the greatest general of his time. Victor over the Persians, the Ostrogoths, and the Vandals, conqueror of Africa and Italy, he had led back captive kings to Justinian's feet, had brought back to Constantinople in triumph the treasures of Genseric and of Theodoric, and had doubled the extent of the empire.

After the fall of Carthage he was given a celebration in the Hippodrome that revived the last recollection of the vanished glories of ancient Rome. Under the eyes of the cheering crowd, he paraded for hours the arms surrendered by Africa at his command, the golden thrones, the precious vases, the heaps of precious stones, the priceless table services, the magnificent garments, the ornate vehicles, the long columns of captive barbarians with their unkempt savage hair. Among them was Gelimer, once more robed in his royal purple, striding behind, downcast, melancholy, and bitter.

From his triumphal chariot Belisarius threw liberally to the mobs jars of silver coins, purses of gold pieces, and coins by the handful bearing the likeness of the emperor.

Constantinople, in gratitude, raised gold statues to Belisarius, and to celebrate "the glory of Rome" it joined the image of Belisarius with that of Justinian on the commemorative medals it struck.

After the fall of Ravenna, Constantinople resounded for weeks with the splendor of Belisarius's renown. When he rode through the streets to report to the Sacred Palace, followed by a picturesque escort of Gothic, Persian, Moorish, and Vandal soldiers, the crowds never stopped adoring his tall stature, his kindly countenance, his bold and noble bearing. They praised his virtues, his courage, his victories. They applauded him, they pressed close to him to salute him, to speak to him. Amiable, receptive, he let them do it, with a kind greeting for everyone. In the midst of his seven thousand guardsmen, loyally devoted to his person, he looked, at the height of his career, like an all-powerful king reentering his capital.

He was the idol of his soldiers and of the people. His troops adored the magnificent gallantry that made him charge at the head of his squadrons like an ordinary cavalryman, and also his always ready generosity and the liberality with which he distributed money and rewards to them. It was thought an unparalleled honor to be attached to his staff. The bravest of the vanquished were proud to serve him. To earn praises from him, his guardsmen would brave any peril, and they would even be happy to sacrifice their lives for him.

The provincials admired him for the restraint he imposed on his soldiers, the attention he gave to his rule over their territory, and his eagerness to see them fairly paid for the supplies he requisitioned.

At Constantinople people forgot the bloody severity with which Belisarius had repressed the Nika uprising and, remembering only his victories, proclaimed him the greatest general in the world. Even his opponents bowed to his eminent qualities. His presence itself at the head of his troops seemed a sure guaranty of their success. His name alone was worth a victory.

He could easily have become king over the Italy he

conquered and reigned over the Goths he had just fought, who all, as good judges of military valor, offered him their throne as their conqueror.

Surrounded by a shining aura, rich as a king, Belisarius seemed to be the real master of the empire. "I do not believe," said a contemporary, "that anyone would have dared to oppose any order he might have given; everyone would have been eager to obey him, as much out of respect for his virtues as out of fear of his might."

Belisarius took part in all important affairs of state. He was the counselor most listened to at the palace, where it was realized he was powerful enough to do what he chose. He was the most-sought-after man in Byzantium.

At the same time, without wishing to, without even thinking it, Belisarius made all those uneasy who sat in the seats of power. John of Cappadocia loathed him, seeing in him a rival for his influence. Theodora disliked him almost as much, fearing a day might come when he might be tempted to risk ousting the government. Justinian, in spite of the relative confidence he reposed in this friend of his youth, sometimes feared he saw in him his successor. There was, in fact, a wide-spread belief in the capital that Belisarius was only waiting for an opportune moment to overthrow the regime.

Fortunately for the emperor, Belisarius was in no sense a political being. He was a simple soldier, loyal and true. He would never have wished to be anything other. A compatriot of the emperor, attached to him personally even before Justinian's accession, he felt more tightly bound to him than most of his subjects. When Justinian demanded of him that while Justinian lived he would never aspire to the throne, he was happy to vow it sincerely.

Besides, his character never inspired ambitious dreams in him. Sensible of honors, of external glory, of popularity, he never asked for the realities of the exercise of political power. He was embarrassed by having to stand in the front rank. A brave soldier, a good general, he rather lacked, out-side matters relating to his own profession, original ideas or initiative. Born to carry out the orders of others, to serve rather than to lead, he wished to be only an efficient servitor, an obedient instrument of the emperor's will. Very respect-ful of the constituted powers, he was a willing and humble subject. Sometimes his greatness embarrassed him, and to make amends for it he often lowered himself even more than was necessary.

He knew that the empress only barely approved him. To disarm her hostility, he took the trouble to work for her, even in rather demeaning errands. He knew Justinian was jealous of his glory, his fortune, his prestige. He went out of his way, out of an excess of consideration, to reassure his friend.

This soldier who, on the battlefield, showed such ex-emplary gallantry, was lacking in civil courage. For years he was apprehensive of Theodora's dislike, even more fear-ful of tangling with her. For years, to maintain her favor at court, he allowed himself too obligingly to be dragged into female intrigues. He was a hero in a time of decadence, not all of a piece, not like tempered steel.

All his life he allowed himself, unprotesting, to be slandered, denounced, and humiliated. He said nothing if he encountered double-dealing or disfavor. Nor was he spared.

While Belisarius was in Italy, the suspicious palace sta-tioned spies even on his staff. They reported back to Con-stantinople, misrepresenting every step he took, even the most innocent. With his army in Italy he was given Narses, Theodora's confidential agent, as a colleague—or rather as an informer armed with a commission that authorized him to countermand any order the general gave. Three or four times, without good reason, Belisarius was relieved of his command. They almost went so far as to deprive him of his headquarters staff and to confiscate a part of his possessions.

After his first campaign in Italy, which ended so success-fully, Belisarius was refused the honor of a triumph in the capital. After the second, they created an impossible situa-tion in which his military prestige was permanently lowered. This is why Theodora considered it essential to apply ex-ceptional measures to hold Belisarius firmly and constantly to his loyalty and duty. For this purpose she made use of the best instrument she had to hand: she used Antonina.

If we can believe the *Secret History*, Antonina, like Theodora, had a pretty stormy youth. She was the daughter of a circus charioteer and a professional prostitute. She led a licentious life at first. Then it seems she married into quite a modest station in life and had several children, among them a son, Photius. She lost her husband, then met Beli-sarius and made a conquest of him, though she was then not exactly young. She was about forty when Justinian came to the throne.

Belisarius married her and loved her passionately all his life. It was a love affair the gossips of Byzantium could explain only, as was their custom, by accusing Antonina of the practice of magic. In any case, Belisarius adored her to the point of madness—or even worse, of weakness. He was unable to bear being away from her. He took her along with him on his campaigns, to Africa, to Asia Minor, to Italy, and always allowed her to sit in on his councils of war.

For Antonina's sake Belisarius would sacrifice the most momentous military moves. For her sake he would lend him-self to the most shady female intrigues. To satisfy her whims, her tastes, or her dislikes, nothing was too much for him. Even his best friends were shocked at the excess of a passion that was more imperative than conjugal. Completely under the influence of his wife, he always listened to her and never acted behind her back.

It must be said that Antonina was exceedingly intelli-gent, capable of courage and of giving sound advice. During the siege of Rome, she was cool enough to cross the lines of the besiegers, with no more protection than a weak escort of cavalry, to hurry the arrival of relief. During the second Italian campaign, she took part in the attack that was aimed at lifting the blockade of the Eternal City. Her inventive mind applied itself to even the smallest detail. During the long voyage of the squadron that was conveying the army of Belisarius to Africa, she was the only one who found a way of serving potable water to the general. She buried large clay jars of water in sand down in the lower hold, safe from the hot rays of the sun.

Antonina always showed herself attentively careful of her husband's best interests—with which her own were bound up, to be sure. To get him the reinforcements he needed, she never hesitated to make the long voyage from Italy to Constantinople. She put to work all the influence she had at court for her husband's benefit.

Theodora soon realized that having a hold on Antonina gave her a hold on Belisarius, though at first Theodora had little taste for Antonina. Theodora even disliked her cordiality. Possibly her dislike was for the scandalous affairs by which that passionate woman rapidly made her spouse, Belisarius, look ridiculous. It may be so. Possibly Theodora feared that Antonina might give him ideas that might endanger Justinian's throne. It is true that Antonina was a schemer to the utmost degree, clever enough to see difficult machinations through successfully, and free of any kind of scruples. She was ambitious as well, avid for power and influence, and unquestionably much bolder and more intelligent than Belisarius. One might well dread that such a woman might one day cause the patrician to deviate from his loyalty to the crown. Theodora devoted herself to getting Antonina in her power, so that through her she could control Belisarius.

Antonina unwittingly gave Theodora the opportunity she was awaiting. When, on 22 June 533, the Byzantine fleet was leaving Constantinople to sail to Africa, the patriarch

Epiphanius, to invoke the blessing of heaven on the holy enterprise, sent along on the admiral's ship a newly converted young soldier, only just baptized the day before. He was Theodosius, who had for some time been in service in the home of Belisarius. The patrician and his wife had stood as godparents for Theodosius, and by reason of this religious parentage they regarded him as their adopted son.

It did not take long for Antonina to become even more actively interested in him. During the boredom of the long voyage she became very much taken with the young man. She became enamoured of him, and, being a woman unhampered by any scruples, she soon made him her lover.

At first she carried on her love affair discreetly. Later she paraded her affection for Theodosius more openly. The servants all knew of it. Belisarius was the only one who did not. But one day at Carthage, he came on the lovers in a lower room of the palace in a state of undress that could leave no room for doubt. He flew into a violent rage. But Antonina coolly explained: "We were just about," she insisted, "this young man and I, to hide here in the cellar some precious objects taken as booty to keep them from falling into the emperor's hands." The patrician loved money. He loved his wife even more, so he allowed himself to be persuaded. He preferred not to believe the evidence of his own eyes.

Encouraged by his blindness, Antonina lost all restraint. When Belisarius left Africa to return to Constantinople, and a year later when he set out for Sicily, Antonina took her lover along everywhere. She even worked on her husband's weakness to have Theodosius named major domo of the patrician's civilian establishment.

At Syracuse she caused a scandal by the openness with which she carried on her love affair. But nobody around her dared to say a word about it. The weakness of Belisarius for his wife was well known. Nobody cared to run the risk of exposing himself to Antonina's venomous retaliation. Every-

body reckoned it would be safer and more prudent to remain on good terms with her than to enlighten her husband.

One chambermaid, Macedonia, probably because of
some quarrel she had with her mistress, decided to disclose
his misfortune to Belisarius under the seal of secrecy. To
confirm her denunciation she brought along two slaves in
Antonina's personal domestic service. The patrician was
furious. He at once ordered that Theodosius be killed. But
the guards charged with carrying out this decree thought
they should forewarn the young man. He was able to take
flight and made off to seek asylum in the sanctuary at
Ephesus.

As for the clever Antonina, she was able once more to
extricate herself from this dilemma. She persuaded Belisarius that she was the victim of an odious slander. She had
little difficulty in satisfying him of her innocence. After that,
to avoid a recurrence of such accidents, she demanded that
her husband deliver over her accusers to her. The overly
gossipy chambermaid and the two faithless slaves had their
tongues cut out. Then, sewn up into sacks, they were thrown
into the sea.

There were other adversaries also in the group around
Belisarius whom Antonina treated with equal cruelty. Constantine, one of the officers on the general staff, was so indiscreet as to say: "As for me, I would have let the lover go,
but I would have killed the woman." Antonina never forgave this. With devilish patience, little by little she reduced
Belisarius's confidence in Constantine. As the officer was
himself extremely proud and inclined to be rude, she found
it easy to embroil the two men. Besides, during the campaign in Italy Constantine had made the mistake of
confiscating some precious objects taken from a prominent
resident of Ravenna, one Praesidius, and refusing all suggestions from his general that he return them.

The patrician's patience came to an end. Irritated, he
demanded that, if the officer persisted in his refusal to obey

and held out, he would call the guards. "No doubt you wish to kill me," exclaimed Constantine, who knew the hatred Antonina felt for him, and without waiting for more, he drew his dagger and threatened Belisarius with it. He was arrested, thrown into prison, and put to death in his dungeon. Antonina was revenged.

His wife's complaint about Constantine reminded Belisarius about Theodosius. But Theodosius was not to be seen.

The patrician had brought Antonina's son, Photius, with him in the army to Italy and treated that young man with marked affection. Now Photius detested Theodosius, whom he suspected of having a love affair with his mother and whom he also disliked for the favor Belisarius showed him. Theodosius does not seem to have been personally too courageous and declared that he would not return to army headquarters as long as Photius remained close to the general.

Between her son and her lover, Antonina had no hesitancy. She connived so well that Photius, bored, disgusted, and weary of being shunted off into trifling assignments, got himself sent back to Constantinople. Then, behind the easygoing complacency of Belisarius, Theodosius and Antonina resumed their love affair. Later, after the fall of Ravenna, when the general returned to Constantinople, Antonina returned to the capital in triumph, this time accompanied by both her husband and her lover.

Theodora soon learned about this intrigue that had been going on for seven years and about which everyone talked openly. Antonina knew that the empress had knowledge of all her affairs. It was this that drew the two women together. To avoid incurring the sovereign's ill will, Antonina put all her skills at the empress's disposal. She had had the good fortune, while she was in Italy, to aid in the downfall of Theodora's enemy Pope Silverius. Theodora appreciated Antonina's know-how, and understood well that, in protecting Antonina's love affairs she was making of Antonina a devoted instrument for her own policy and a sure guaranty of the loyalty of Belisarius to Justinian.

United by this community of interest, they grew very close to each other. Antonina became Theodora's favorite companion, intimate friend, and confidante. Theodora appointed her to the high post of grand mistress of the empress's household. Secure in her good fortune, Antonina would deny Theodora nothing.

Theodosius, however, began to feel uneasy about a love affair carried on so publicly. Possibly this was also partly because he began to weary of a mistress who was so demanding. Once more, he went away. But this time, to get some peace, he entered a monastery. Antonina fell into deep despair. She would see no one and practically went into mourning. Bathed in tears, she never stopped moaning, even in the presence of Belisarius, about the amiable, the faithful, the charming friend she had lost. She made such a fuss that her well-meaning husband asked Justinian and Theodora for an interview, and, asserting that he could not get along without the services of his indispensable servitor Theodosius, he begged Justinian to order Theodosius to return.

Belisarius did even more for Antonina. As he was about to leave to take command of the army on the Persian front, he agreed, contrary to his standing custom, to allow Antonina to remain behind in the capital. As soon as he had left, Theodosius, who had strongly protested that he did not wish to leave his monastery, was forced to leave it and rejoin his mistress in Constantinople. Antonina's passion had made her reckless.

Left to himself and open to the influence of others, Belisarius at last had his eyes opened. It was Photius who took it on himself to enlighten his stepfather. Braving the hatred of his mother, who tried to compromise him with his general and who even considered, it was said, having him done away with, he played an important role. He proved to Belisarius how shamelessly his wife had played on his steadfast weakness for her.

This time, feeling he was fully justified, the general really took umbrage. He asked Photius to help him avenge his outraged honor. Yet, even at that decisive moment, he could not bring himself to cut himself off from Antonina. "I am still in love with my wife," he confessed, "even if I punish the man who has dishonored my home. I cannot wish to do her harm, but I cannot forgive Theodosius for what he has done."

In spite of this reservation, in spite of the lack of vigor behind the decision of Belisarius, Photius agreed to serve in this cause. The two men exchanged solemn vows on the holy scriptures not to betray each other and to brave the consequences even to the death. Then they awaited a favorable occasion.

This was in 541. Antonina had just rendered Theodora a signal service. She had been the heart of the scheme that had ousted John of Cappadocia, so her standing with Theodora had risen accordingly. She felt, therefore, that she ran no danger if she sent her lover back to Ephesus and rejoined her husband. So she set out for the army headquarters. Contrary to her expectations, she found Belisarius highly exasperated.

As soon as he heard his wife had arrived, Belisarius forgot the higher interests of the state and evacuated the Persian territory he had lately overrun, in his hurry to concentrate on his personal affairs. For the first time in his life he gave Antonina a cold reception. He put a secret guard over her, and, it was rumored, even thought of killing her.

At the same time Photius cross-examined one of his mother's eunuchs and learned where Theodosius had taken refuge. With the complicity of the local bishop, he bodily snatched Antonina's lover out of the Church of Saint John at

Ephesus. He laid violent hands on the favorite's luck and transferred him under heavy guard to a castle far away in Cilicia.

Belisarius and Photius had timed their move badly. Theodora was unwilling to allow her friend to be harmed. Most annoyed with what had been done to Antonina, she at once had Belisarius summoned back to Constantinople. We have already learned how Theodora took revenge on Photius and his accomplices for the offense he had given Antonina, and with what cool audacity she restored, to Antonina's delight, the cherished lover to her favorite. At the same time she worked on reconciling Belisarius to his wife. The deep love the general felt for his wife had, even before his return to the capital, begun to soften his feelings. Seeing his determination melt away so rapidly, the gossips of Constantinople, who were following this tragicomedy with great curiosity, wondered what sort of spell had been cast on the poor man.

Theodora found it not too difficult to reconcile the spouses. The general did not have to be persuaded. But what happened then? Theodosius suddenly died, and the empress's request to Belisarius became academic. He took Antonina back, and she, with cruel unconcern, never even bothered to ask what happened to Photius and his friends.

To please the empress, Belisarius let himself be made to look a coward and an oath breaker. He came out of the affair much diminished in stature. Yet, he did retain a vague resentment against the two women who had humiliated him.

Belisarius was returned to his command in 542, but he carried on his military operations negligently, and, it was whispered, allowed himself to listen to some of the seditious plans that offended Theodora so profoundly. The empress concluded that she had to teach him a lesson. He was abruptly relieved of his command and again ordered back to Constantinople, where he was required to pay over all the money he owned to a eunuch sent by the empress and to surrender to the enemy all the members of his personal bodyguard because their loyalty was in question.

The sovereigns received him coldly. He was ostracized by his friends, who avoided being compromised by him. Belisarius seemed to be in complete disgrace. It was a lamentable spectacle to see the great general now, running through the streets unattended, avoided by all, somber and worried, constantly fearing for his life and imagining himself already surrounded by assassins.

Nevertheless, Antonina remained high in favor at the palace. She was the bosom friend, and indispensable companion of the empress. Since the affair of the year before, she was only on cool terms with her husband. Theodora very wisely advised her, however, to effect a full reconciliation with him, reckoning that if Belisarius would owe a full pardon and a reentry into favor to Antonina, it would make him the slave, from then on and forever, of her who had saved him.

Then one day, in accordance with custom, Belisarius was presented at an imperial audience, encountering faces especially hostile and frozen. What was worse, he was exposed to insults and abuse from the rabble of servants at court. Returning home that evening, more and more upset over his fate, he lay down on his couch trembling with fear, without courage or dignity. Antonina was there, complaining that she was not feeling well and striding about the room. Night fell. Suddenly there was a violent knocking at the door. "An order from the empress," called out a servant from the palace.

Belisarius, thinking his last hour had come, stood up, ready to receive the fatal blow. Instead of a message of doom, it was a letter from Theodora the servant had brought. This is what it said: "You know, my friend, what you have done to displease us. But I am under great obligation to your wife. Because of her I have decided to forgive you. I want you to know that you owe your life to her. It is only to her you can look in the future if you hope for your survival and fortune. We shall see by events whether you conduct yourself properly with her."

Antonina, who was fully aware of the contents of the letter, awaited its effect with interest. It was prodigious. Overjoyed, Belisarius rose. To give the messenger from the empress immediate proof of his obedience, he fell excitedly at Antonina's feet, kissed her hands, folded her in his arms, and swore that in the future he would be not only her husband but her devoted slave.

This was the price he paid to obtain the return of a part of his fortune, the restitution of his honors, and an important military assignment. He was sent to Italy, but without an army, without funds, and without supplies. It was said he even had to pay the cost of this expedition out of his own funds.

It is not easy to sort out how much is hard fact in these stories. Was Belisarius actually partly to blame for Antonina's conduct by his complacency? After a short burst of determination, did he really resume this complacency to return to favor and earn the good opinion of the empress? These are the tales of gossips we can hardly credit. One can well believe that, as Antonina was Theodora's favorite, Belisarius refrained from tangling with his sovereign out of fear. In any case, it seems to be established that he made use of Antonina to assure his standing at the palace. On the other hand, it is equally certain that he was madly in love with her.

On the second expedition into Italy, when the objective was to save Rome, he wept like a child when news was brought him that his wife had fallen into the hands of the Ostrogoths. To save her, he retreated and abandoned everything. One can believe he was glad to indulge her. Even after Theodora's death he continued blindly to submit to her influence.

However all that may be, it was thought in Constantinople that Belisarius, as soon as he left the capital, would have his revenge for his humiliations and his disgrace by lending himself to an insurrection. Exactly the opposite happened. Antonina accompanied him to Italy. Her presence sufficed to hold him to his duty. Always ready to serve the will of the empress, she showed herself, as long as she lived, absolutely the servant of Theodora's will, and Theodora, in return, never begrudged her protection. Thus, the design of the empress was successful. In attaching Antonina to herself, she tied Belisarius to Justinian's interests.

Theodora hoped, thanks to her favorite, to realize an even lovelier dream. Belisarius was prodigiously rich. He loved money, and he had no scruples about how he amassed it. It was suspected with good reason that a large part of his wealth, too large, consisted of booty from Africa and Italy and gifts he had accepted from enemies of Pope Silverius for having been his executioner. It is certain that he did not hesitate to accept the luxurious palace of John of Cappadocia as recompense for the part Antonina had played in the downfall of that favorite. However he got it, his fortune was, as one contemporary phrased it, worthy of an emperor.

Justinian and Theodora had been quite anxious to get their hands on it, but partly out of consideration for the public services Belisarius had given and possibly because of lacking a plausible excuse, they had not dared to go so far as complete confiscation. They even were careful not to point out that a good part of his riches had probably been acquired at the expense of the treasury. In any case, the empress believed she could achieve the same result by other means.

Belisarius had an only daughter, Joan, who was to inherit this unparalleled fortune. Theodora planned to marry Joan to her grandson, Athanasius. This alliance was one of the conditions the empress insisted on in the peace she struck with the general at the time of his relief from deep disgrace. In spite of his repugnance to it, the patrician had consented to announcing the engagement.

But once he got away to Italy, he regained his poise, and unexpectedly he won the support of Antonina in objecting to it. Possibly she felt that the empress, who was then ill and on the verge of a decline, or for other reasons, could not enforce the pact, so she could resist the sovereign's wishes.

The empress wrote letter after letter demanding that they get on with the marriage ceremony, but to no avail. The parents advanced a hundred pretexts to put it off, first urging it must await their return to Constantinople, then arguing other reasons for postponing that return.

Theodora was much disturbed. She suspected that, if she were to die, Antonina might conveniently forget both the promise she had made and the gratitude she owed her protectress. She decided to speed up events.

She threw the young people together in such fashion that soon the marriage ceremony was no more than a necessary formality. Athanasius and Joan were so smitten with each other that, with the sovereign's complicity, they began to live together. Their intimacy had lasted eight months when Theodora died.

A little later Antonina returned to Constantinople. Her reaction proved at once how right Theodora had been about her. Forgetting all about the past, she would hear no more of the proposed union. Although her daughter's reputation was seriously blemished by the involvement, and without allowing herself to be disturbed by the despair of the two young lovers, Antonina separated them brutally, declaring she would never accept a descendant of Theodora's as a son-in-law. When Belisarius returned from Italy somewhat later, he naturally approved, as he always did, what Antonina had decided.

Although on this one point Theodora's death ruined the plans she had laid, the line of conduct she had dictated with regard to Belisarius was obediently followed, even after her departure. To his last day the general was under suspicion of striving too hard for popularity and of nourishing hopes that were overly ambitious. Although heaping honors on him, Justinian did not spare him humiliation, even disgrace, in his old age.

Almost the very next day after the patrician Belisarius, in rendering a supreme service, had saved the capital and the emperor from an attack by the Huns, the restless jealousy of Justinian charged him with being implicated in a conspiracy against the sovereign. Nothing like this was proven, yet the emperor, in a violent scene, gave vent to his anger against Belisarius. Once more Belisarius was deprived of his bodyguard, stripped of all his honors and commands, and subjected to house arrest in his palace. Theodora's mind continued to direct Justinian's actions against this redoubtable subject of the crown.

Yet, in respect to the memory of the empress, Justinian continued to show favor to Antonina, who had been Theodora's confidante and closest friend. Until her death Antonina continued to win recognition at the palace. The policy by which Theodora had made the general's establishment feel the effect of her power was continued, so that, in this again, it survived her death.

Until the end, Belisarius, in obedience to Antonina, remained the humble, docile, and faithful servant of Justinian's will.

15

Theodora's Feminism

If one can credit the *Secret History*, Theodora showed inexhaustible patience with the weaknesses of others. She was a woman who knew all about life and recognized the frailty of human nature.

In a great city like Constantinople morals were far from irreproachable. Adultery was common, homes torn by dissension were not at all unusual. The empress spread her mantle over all this complacently.

Should a married woman have a lover and be indiscreet enough to let it be discovered, she would run posthaste to the palace, and, always with the sovereign's support, extricate herself from her predicament.

Bad luck for the husband if, in suing for divorce, he failed to produce irrefutable proof of his charges in court. He would be sentenced to pay his wife an amount equal to the dowry she had brought him. He would run the risk of flogging and imprisonment, while the lady, secure in her impunity, would openly boast of her adultery. Many injured husbands deemed it wiser to shut their eyes. Thanks to Theodora, the capital became thoroughly demoralized.

If, in view of these goings-on, we consider the information we gather from official documents, we must confess that, much to the contrary, the Sacred Palace prided itself on its prudery. A very large proportion of Justinian's laws dealt with marriage, divorce, and adultery. Ever again, the phrase that the emperor's greatest concern was for public morals was repeated. "We wish," he wrote somewhere, "that women behave themselves properly, that they not lead an irregular or irreligious life. We hope they will attain this goal."

It is instructive to note how many acts the emperor regarded as the opposite of moral and good behavior.

If a woman was so shameless as to go to the baths during men's hours, her husband could demand a divorce from her. If, without permission from her husband, she went out to dine with strangers, or if, without her husband's knowledge or in spite of his objection, she went to the theater, to the races, or to animal fights—any of these acts was recognized by the law as ground for divorce.

Even stronger, it was good ground for throwing her out if a woman spent a night away from the conjugal domicile, or if during her spouse's lifetime she planned another marriage, or above all if she took a lover.

In case the husband came upon his wife and her seducer together either in his own home or the lover's, in a tavern or somewhere in the outskirts, he had the right, after three preliminary warnings, to administer justice himself. If he came on them by surprise elsewhere, for instance in church (as the church often served as the place for a tryst), he could deliver the couple to the public authorities, and, if the case was clear, the lover was condemned to death without a formal trial and the wife sent back to her husband to be punished according to law.

The law was not at all tender to the female adulteress. After her divorce she was to be shut up in a convent and if, after two years, her husband would not consent to take her back, she was to be tonsured and kept in the convent for the rest of her days.

As Justinian wrote somewhere, to strengthen the institution of marriage, "that state holier than all others," to surround it with all the safeguards and preserve it "durable and indissoluble" was his primary preoccupation. He forbade divorce by consent of the parties as being too easy to break the sacred tie. He reduced the number of grounds for divorce, characterizing as ill-founded many of those previously allowed by the ancient laws. He did not believe imprisonment of one of the spouses, or imposition of certain penalties, to be a sufficient reason for dissolving the union. He refused to permit the wife of a soldier to consider herself free to remarry merely because she was left without news of her husband; she had to present formal proof of his death. He promulgated the severest penalties against those who manufactured pretexts to justify separation in order to enable them to lead a looser life.

Only the desire to enter the religious life found favor in his eyes as a ground for divorce, but it had to be shown that the call was serious and permanent. The law severely punished any who left the convent to resume life in the world.

I am well aware that, at all times and in every country, the law and the practice of domestic relations are not necessarily in accord. The severity of Justinian's legislation, however, inclines me to believe that on this point, as on so many others, the *Secret History* has, to some extent, slandered Theodora. What is true, and it is possible that here we must recognize her influence, is that the status of woman in marriage was ameliorated in many respects.

The wife was protected against mistreatment and capricious whims of the husband. She could demand a divorce for notorious misconduct by him, "a circumstance that," as Justinian pointed out, "is particularly offensive to women, especially to those who conduct themselves properly," or if her husband tried to tempt her into debauchery. Beyond this, she need not fear to be cast out without good reason or to be falsely accused of adultery.

In such cases the law required convincing proof and permitted the wife, if the accusation was seen to be slanderous, to demand the divorce herself, without prejudice to the money damages and the other penalties to which the husband could be sentenced.

The husband could not beat his wife without entirely legitimate justification. He could not, without good grounds, eject her from his home, and the law added, with some touch of humor, that if a night she was so forced to spend away from home resulted in some embarrassing consequence, the husband had no one to blame for it but himself.

In spite of this salutary and well-meaning intervention by Theodora in behalf of wives mistreated or unhappily married, she had, as did Justinian, great respect herself for the sanctity of marriage and was herself a stern guardian of public morals, as the facts prove.

Artabanus was a handsome Armenian officer, of fine appearance and good breeding. Related to the royal family of the Arsacides, he had come to seek his fortune in the Byzantine Empire. By his courage, his firm will, and his generous nature, he had rapidly become popular all through the army.

He was in Africa when the military uprising broke out in which Areobindus was killed. He felt a chivalrous regard for the young widow, whom events had delivered into the hands of the revolutionaries. She was a niece of Justinian, Prejecta by name. The ambitious Armenian hoped to draw some advantage from services he might render so great a lady.

He was not mistaken. Having been saved by him, Prejecta could refuse her liberator nothing. Not satisfied with showering wealth on him, she soon promised him her hand. Already Artabanus, intoxicated with his good fortune, saw himself on the way to the throne, thanks to such a brilliant marriage.

All went as he hoped. Prejecta returned to Constantinople, and Justinian, to be agreeable to the young lovers, authorized Artabanus to follow her there. To shorten the distance that separated the young man from the object of his affection, Justinian covered him with dignities and honors. He made him commander-in-chief of one of the foreign contingents of guards, commander of the militia, and a consul.

But then someone started trouble. Artabanus had completely forgotten that long ago, somewhere in Armenia, he had contracted a marriage, though it had been so long ago that he had parted from his first wife and he had heard nothing about her since. Now, however, she suddenly turned up in Constantinople. Claiming her rights as his lawful spouse, she found she had a strong supporter in the empress.

Theodora was inflexible in a matter that concerned the preservation of the sacred bonds of matrimony. She forced Artabanus, regardless of whatever he had in mind to do, to take back his wife. Then out of excess of precaution, she married off Prejecta to someone else.

She was just as strict in her care for the preservation of good morals, as she showed in the case of two young women of high position who became widows and too easily found consolation for the loss of their husbands. Their conduct came to the knowledge of the empress. She felt it was a bad example to others. She made up her mind they must remarry. To punish them for their arrogance and to humiliate them, Theodora produced suitors of quite humble origin for them.

Shocked, the two sisters took refuge in the Church of Saint Sophia, counting on being able there to avoid such distasteful unions. But Theodora insisted. They had to give in, and although men of their own rank were asking for their hands, each acquiesced against her will to marriage beneath her. But it must be added that, with this accomplished, the empress made it her business to console her victims. She actively saw to the advancement of the new husbands and covered them with favors and honors.

It may be that with her dictatorial disposition and her way of subordinating everything else to the objectives of her policies, Theodora may sometimes have been too meddlesome in family and household affairs that did not actually concern her. She has been criticized for forcing marriages with the same despotism she applied to the running of the government, for joining and separating couples without even consulting them, just because it pleased her to do so.

We have seen how she worked to prevent the marriage of the daughter of Germanus and how she did her best to arrange one for the daughter of Belisarius. These were not merely pastimes for her indulgence. In doing what she did, Theodora was serving her political designs.

In the same way, when she made Prejecta marry a nephew of that same Hypatius whom long ago the Nika uprising had proclaimed emperor, her objective beyond everything else was to reduce the potential of an aspirant to the throne. It was for reasons of the same high order that she first covered up Antonina's amours for her and later urged her to effect a reconciliation with Belisarius.

When Theodora's interests were at stake no moral scruples weighed on her in the least. Apparently it was the same when she determined to help relatives or friends. We know how she worked out fine marriages for her sister Comito and her niece, Sophia. She accomplished as much for her intimate friend Chrysomallo by marrying her daughter to Saturninus, the son of Hermogenes, master of the offices.

The young man was engaged to marry one of his relatives, a girl of good family, pretty and innocent. Theodora ruthlessly broke off this plan for marriage and forced Saturninus to accept Chrysomallo's daughter. The wedding took place, but after the wedding night Saturninus complained bitterly to his friends that he had not found his bride intact. This was his mistake. Theodora had him arrested and flogged, to teach him, she said, not to gossip so freely.

It seems that still other forced marriages were Theodora's handiwork. It is worth keeping in mind that we do not have much information about the results of such episodes. They did not all turn out so well.

In all these instances Theodora did not concern herself much about the man. She, always acting the woman, was "naturally inclined to come to the aid of women in misfortune," according to the phrase of a historian.

That is how she acted particularly in the measures she

inspired Justinian to adopt for the relief of actresses and lost women. She knew the lower depths of the capital from having come through them herself. She knew what misery and shame they generated. Very early she began to use her influence to remedy this.

I am willing to believe it was to her that Justinian made a discreet allusion when in one of his decrees for the reform of bad morals, he spoke of "a person" who had for a long time kept him informed of the corruption in Constantinople, and that it was she who instigated the official investigations that resulted in the framing of a number of laws to correct and control it.

In any case I can believe that Theodora helped to free actresses from that socially inferior status in which they had been kept, either by permitting them to leave the profession, if they chose, or by breaking down the last barriers that stood in the way of a respectable marriage.

Up to that time it had been the general custom in the Byzantine theater to force girls against their will, when they entered the theatrical profession, to sign contracts binding them never to leave it, as a matter of precaution by their employers. Later the law nullified these contracts as immoral. The actresses were empowered to cancel these vows, on the ground that in the eyes of the Lord this was not an act chargeable as perjury. Under threat of severe penalties, orders were given to bishops and to governors of provinces to take care to assure actresses of their freedom, and to refer any case in which they were powerless to have the law respected to the emperor.

Severe penalties were to be enacted against theater managers who tried to insist on such unconscionable contracts—not only confiscation of their possessions and exile, but they were to be subjected to a fine of ten gold pounds (about $2,200 in our money) to be paid to a complainant to enable her to live honestly.

Being in this manner enabled to reenter a normal life, actresses could contract a marriage with even the most highly placed dignitaries without their having to apply for an imperial license to do so, just as Justin had previously decreed to facilitate the marriage of his nephew Justinian. The same privilege was extended to their daughters. The only obligation imposed on them was that, in such cases, they must never go back to the stage.

It was near to Theodora's heart, as the official guardian of public morals, to make her capital a moral city. We know what a notorious part was played in it by the criminal industry of procurers, and how many unfortunate girls they enticed with handsome promises into houses of ill fame. We have seen how widely the bordellos were scattered in Constantinople and by what shameful contracts the victims of this deplorable traffic were tied to them, often in spite of themselves. Theodora wished to put all this in order.

An imperial decree made it illegal and punishable by death to entice a young girl, in spite of herself, into a life of debauchery. It was made illegal to operate a house of prostitution. Those in operation were ordered to close their houses and pay back to the girls who were shut up in them the money these girls had been made to deposit as security. Finally, procurers were expelled from the city as "detrimental to the community, and corrupters of public morals." The decree of the emperor read: "We ordain that all our subjects, as many as there may be, shall from now on behave properly. Good conduct is the best recommendation to God for the soul of man."

Theodora herself kept watch on the enforcement of the measures she had urged. She made it her business, as one of the chroniclers says, to free poor girls lost "under the yoke of their shameful slavery." By her orders the procurers of the capital and their victims were summoned to a meeting where they were made to disclose, under oath, how much money they had given the parents of these miserable girls. On learning they had paid an average of $1320 for each, the empress redeemed all these unfortunates out of her own funds, gave each in addition a decent garment and $330 and sent them home to their families.

Theodora founded an institution for those who were cut off by their families. On the Asian side of the Bosporus in an old imperial palace, she founded the Convent of Metanoia (which means repentance) for repentant girls. To protect these unfortunates from temptation that in the past their needs had often forced on them, she endowed this charity richly.

It is said that some of these new recluses adjusted very badly to this sudden change in their way of life and chose to throw themselves to death from the top of their prison walls. It may be so, but this does not derogate from the honor due Theodora. These words in the imperial decree that she doubtless inspired Justinian to issue express remarkable dignity: "We have appointed magistrates to punish robbers and those who steal money. Is there not better reason to pursue those who steal one's honor and rob her of chastity?"

We may be confident that in all this legislation and in her natural sympathy for women in misfortune, Theodora was moved by some recollection and some regret for her past. If she did not actually speak the words, she must have thought as the poet who wrote: "Having known misfortune, I know how to aid the unfortunate."

It is quite probable that she did think this way, even if we cannot be certain of it, and this is not meant to color any image of Theodora we wish to make for ourselves. That former theater dancer who climbed to the throne of the Caesars was by no means unworthy of her good fortune. She rose from the lowest, yet in spite of her faults and her shortcomings, she became a great empress.

Emerging out of a tempestuous youth, she developed, by a strange and unforeseeable contradiction, a love of serious things, a constant concern for public morals, and a consciousness of her own worth.

This mosaic, on the north wall of the sanctuary in the Church of Saint Vitalis at Ravenna, depicts Emperor Justinian in a procession entering the church. Carrying as a gift a large golden paten that is to serve for the celebration of the mass, Justinian is robed in purple. The halo behind his head signifies the power conferred on him by God. To Justinian's left is Archbishop Maximianus, who precedes him into the church. The figure behind the emperor and the archbishop is believed to be either Julianus, the wealthy banker who financed the building of the church, or the Praetorian prefect for Italy. Some authorities believe the figure to the emperor's right may be Belisarius, who conquered Ravenna for Justinian in 540. The Church of Saint Vitalis was completed in 546 and is still intact.

Located on the south wall of the sanctuary in Ravenna's Church of Saint Vitalis, this mosaic portrays Empress Theodora about to enter the church. The apse of the church can be seen behind her. As her gift she carries the precious chalice that is to serve for the celebration of the mass. She is clothed in a wide purple mantle and wears a diadem and a pectoral adorned with precious stones. The color of her costume and the detail of her jewels are shown with realistic exactness. Some scholars have identified the two women following her at her left as Antonina and Giovannina, the wife and the daughter of General Belisarius, who were Theodora's intimate friends. This portrayal is believed to have been completed about 545, or when Theodora was almost fifty.

This ivory panel, in the Christian Civic Museum at Brescia, shows a chariot race in the Hippodrome at Constantinople as it took place in the time of Justinian and Theodora. In the center is the spina around which the race was conducted. Above the spina is the Egyptian obelisk, which still stands today at Istanbul on the site of the old Hippodrome. The *kathisma*, the royal box from which the emperor and his guests watched the proceedings, is shown at the top of the panel.

Shown here is the interior of the Church of Saints Sergius and Bacchus at Istanbul. Preceding the great Church of the Holy Wisdom (Saint Sophia), it was completed in 527 and provided the precedent for the dome that seems to float on columns, independent of the enclosing walls.

This photograph is unusual because it shows, as it looks today, the interior of the great Church of the Holy Wisdom (Saint Sophia) at Istanbul without the Koranic discs installed by the Muslims. Originally built by Constantine when he founded Constantinople in 330, the church was destroyed in the fire during the Nika revolt in 532. It was built anew for Justinian by the great architect Anthemius of Tralles and consecrated in 537. The great dome was injured several years later in an earthquake but was repaired and reconsecrated in 563. It is one of the marvels of world architecture. The Church of the Holy Wisdom, which has been used continuously as a place of worship, became a mosque after the fall of Constantinople to the Turks in 1453.

PART THREE

Theodora
the Saintly

16

Theodora's Piety

Formal religion occupied a prominent place in every aspect of Byzantine life. It ruled an important part of the court protocol to which an empress had to conform in her daily life. The sovereign, robed in purple and gold, took part in all the many formal orthodox public ceremonies. Followed by a glittering retinue to the great churches of Constantinople—to Saint Sophia or the Holy Apostles, to Saint Sergius or Saint Mocius, to the sanctuary of Saint Mary of the Fountain or that of the Virgin of Blachernae— she took part with devotion in all the religious liturgy. Seated on the throne, among her cubiculars and ostiaries, surrounded by a swarm of elaborately gowned ladies-in-waiting and high dignitaries, she joined in prayer or came piously to the foot of the altar, with taper in hand, to kneel there and utter prayers before the sacred relics.

The imperial processions passed endlessly through the streets of the city in the picturesque luxury of their ceremonial uniforms, constantly varied according to the requirements of official protocol.

Sometimes, in formal pomp, they went to dedicate a new church; sometimes to worship some celebrated religious relic and obtain the saint's aid for a miraculous recovery from illness; sometimes to some famous monastery to beg a benediction from a renowned ascetic; sometimes in a solemn service of thanksgiving to praise God for victories accorded by Divine Providence to the armies of the empire; or again, robed in mourning garments and sounding sad laments, to pray to the all-powerful God to abate his anger and put an end to the scourges of epidemic or earthquake by which he was making the capital desolate.

Being firmly persuaded that an emperor must be the chosen of God, entrusted by the special selection of Providence with the direction of human affairs, convinced that in every crisis, in every time of peril, the Lord extends his protecting arm over the emperor and strengthens his courage and is actually present in all the rituals of the cult and the proceedings of the church, the masters of Byzantium can truly be said to have led a pontifical existence.

Justinian derived unusual satisfaction from his participation in such a life. He was extremely devout, even highly superstitious. He believed he was the object of special solicitude on the part of Providence. It gratified him to claim the benefits of numerous miracles that worked in his favor.

He remembered that once when he was grievously ill and the doctors despaired of being able to save him, the two great medical saints, Saint Cosmo and Saint Damien, whose miraculous powers were known and venerated by all Byzantium, descended from heaven on high expressly to cure him when he was in his last agony.

He remembered another time, when he was seriously crippled and nearly paralyzed by rheumatism, he was miraculously restored by the mere touching of sacred relics and the holy oil that flows from the bodies of martyred saints.

Deeply imbued with gratitude, he strove always to show his appreciation to the Lord, who had so generously given him these striking evidences of his protection. It was his ever constant care to preserve the purity of the faith, to defend the church on every occasion, to reform its discipline and its dogma, and to strengthen and spread its influence. He loved to build churches and monasteries. He covered the empire with them.

Justinian liked even better to take an active part himself in theological debates. One of his favorite occupations was to preside at councils of the church, to discuss religious theories with bishops, to argue with dissenters. A good speaker, quite proud of his eloquence, the depth of his learning, and the logic of his reasoning, he believed with some ingenuousness that he had few equals in the skill of disputation, so he took pains to edify church prelates by sermons he spoke, both persuasive and gentle. He was sure he could convert heretics by his irrefutable arguments. He spent whole nights in discussion with learned theologians or composing polemical essays in which he took considerable pride.

All his life he meddled, often indiscreetly, in church affairs. Those who wished to please him complimented him freely on combining in his speech "the mildness of David, the patience of Moses, the mercy of the apostles, and to have brought to pass in his reign the golden age predicted by the prophets when philosophers will be kings and kings philosophers."

Theodora herself had too lively an understanding of the demands of royal etiquette to be wanting in the performance of the pious duties expected of an empress. Besides, she was instinctively shrewd enough in her political sense to realize how important religious questions are in a Christian state and how dangerous it would be not to show interest in them. In any case, she was sincerely pious by instinct. As a good Byzantine, she had great respect for ecclesiastical personages, for monks with their lean bodies in long black garments, and for the holy women who had renounced the world to don "the robes of angels" and become "citizens of heaven."

As were all people of her day, she was profoundly grateful to them for their virtues, their penances, and the prayers through which they supplemented the inadequate merits of other Christians.

Like Justinian, Theodora sincerely admired that monastic life that places man in direct communication with God, that purifies him and gives him strength through meditation, freed from all the common cares of humanity. She loved to surround herself with hermits and ascetics. She received them informally at the Sacred Palace, she discussed spiritual questions with them, willingly granted their requests, and had complete confidence in the efficacy of their intercession.

We have seen how she appealed to the prayers of the Syrian monk Zooras to cure the sick Justinian, and to the great Palestinian saint Sabas to intercede for her in asking the Lord to grant her a son.

The story of her contact with the anchorite Maras is equally pointed and instructive. Maras was one of those fiery Syrians whose intense piety and often uncalculating zeal could not be arrested by any obstacle. When he was about thirty he was suddenly touched by the grace of God on the very day he was to be married. He chose at once to submit to "the less burdensome yoke of the Lord rather than the devastating distractions of a corporeal union."

He entered a monastery where he became notorious for the austerity of his penances and the excessive severity of the mortification to which he subjected his flesh. Overly hard on himself, he was just as severe on others. We know how violently he dared to reprimand Justinian and Theodora to their faces in the Sacred Palace.

This is what impressed the empress so favorably about him. She reasoned that so holy a man must be so close to God as to be most effective in prayer. She invited him to live in the palace. Maras declined.

Then she tried having her treasurer send him a large sum of money as almsgiving. The saint, with insolent scorn, rattled the bag containing the money in his powerful grip and threw the gold pieces back at the empress and her dumbfounded and terrified chamberlain.

This episode made a great stir in the city and at court, but Theodora was not a bit discouraged by it. The saint had withdrawn to the opposite side of the Golden Horn, to the outskirts of Sykae, to be able in quieter solitude to continue the rugged existence to which he had accustomed himself. The empress humbly sent him apologies for having dared to expose him to temptation by her offer. She sent him word that she hoped he would accept at least what he needed for his bare maintenance.

Maras would hear none of it. "There is nothing you have," he stormed, "that the servants of the Lord want of you but that you feel the fear of God if you are capable of doing so." Then, to spare himself further annoyance from imperial entreaties, he moved even further away to find a less accessible retreat.

One night some brigands burst into his tent to attack him. "Hand over the gold the empress sent you," they shouted, "or we will kill you at once." The saint calmly replied: "Believe me, I have no money at all. If I wanted money, I certainly would not be living like this." The robbers, unbelieving, took dagger in hand and one of them struck Maras a blow with a cudgel.

The Syrian was a robust athlete. In a flash he threw his attacker to the ground with a punch, and grasping the stick, he did the same in succession to the other six thieves in the band. He carefully tied them all up and laid their knives and cudgels on the ground beside them. After that he admonished them, with quiet sarcasm: "My sons, I asked you to leave me alone. I regret you paid no attention to me. Now give me the pleasure of lying still until morning. Get it into your heads that you should never scorn even the poorest." Next morning he let them out but kept their daggers and their sticks.

This incident made a terrific impact on the court. When the chamberlain sent to get the story brought it back to the palace and showed the sovereigns the trophies of the saint's victory, Justinian and Theodora were filled with even greater admiration for him than before.

The affair redounded to the Syrian's advantage in another way as well. He consented at last to letting them build him a monastery, where he lived from then on with his disciples, praying and preaching, but not restraining himself any more than before from openly reprimanding the emperor and the empress when he had to.

When in 542 Maras was carried off by the plague, the sovereigns decided to give him a formal state funeral. They sent the most illustrious citizens, the greatest nobles from the palace, cubiculars and senators, bishops, clerics and monks, to attend. The saint's death was regarded as a public calamity in Constantinople.

The proud Theodora had bottomless forbearance for these strange ascetics. Her arrogance bowed to their rebukes, their insolence, their rudeness. Her majesty humbled itself to their tatters. Eager to protect them, she showed them unappeasable generosity. Her charity expended itself in pious benefactions and the founding of monasteries, hospitals, and orphanages. Justinian speaks somewhere of the handsome gifts she made to churches, hospitals, asylums, and to bishops and monks.

She gave the monk Zooras a large plot of ground on the outskirts of Sykae, so he could retire to it with his disciples. So she could offer it as a retirement home to Theodosius, patriarch of Alexandria, she bought a beautiful villa in Thrace at Darkos. She made Jacob Baradaeus accept a completely furnished home in Constantinople. She founded a monastery entirely within the precincts of the Sacred Palace. She had several commodious hostels built to house impoverished strangers whose business brought them to Constantinople.

She constructed basilicas, rest homes for the sick and disabled. She took delight in making munificent gifts to enrich the most illustrious sanctuaries. She loved having her portraits show her in that charitable and liberal posture. We see her with Justinian visiting hospitals and churches on the splendid gold-embroidered tapestry that serves as the communion cloth on the altar at Saint Sophia's. As one contemporary wrote, all were "good works by the masters of the world, these protectors of the city."

Among all these benefactions, the construction of the Church of the Holy Apostles has remained one of the most famous. On the hill where the mosque of Mahomet II today raises its domes surmounted by the crescent, Constantine the Great had built a church dedicated to the holy apostles. His son had ceremoniously transferred to it and placed in a golden casket relics of the apostles Andrew, Luke, and Timothy. The founder of the Christian empire had the hope that this edifice would also serve as a sepulcher for himself and his descendants.

In the time of Justinian the original structure was crumbling with age. The emperor had it demolished. Theodora decided to rebuild it, enlarge it vastly, and make it much more beautiful. In 536 the empress solemnly laid the cornerstone for the new temple. The great architect Anthemius of Tralles, who had then just completed the building of Saint Sophia, supervised the building of the new sanctuary, aided by Isidore the Younger.

As at Saint Sophia, they applied all the splendors and all the resources of Byzantine decoration in the new church. A forest of columns, no doubt removed from pagan temples for the most part, surrounded the exterior of the church in two stories, all in rich colors. On the floor and walls, precious marbles were used in sparkling mosaics. In the vault of the dome and on the walls of the naves, mosaics pictured the principal events in the earthly life of the Savior, and in the center was the figure of Christ triumphant surrounded by his apostles and by the Virgin.

But above all, it is the ground plan of the new structure that is so unique. It is in the form of a Greek cross. While at Saint Sophia one single, enormous dome crowns the edifice, here there are five domes, above the intersection and the ends of the branches of the cross. This arrangement seems to be reminiscent of that of Saint John the Evangelist at

Ephesus. It set a precedent in the history of Byzantine architecture.

While the Saint Sophia structure, which was difficult to copy, has remained unique, the Church of the Holy Apostles, "the new sky with five domes," has served repeatedly as a model for builders in succeeding centuries. Saint Mark at Venice is one replica of the magnificent church built by Justinian and Theodora.

Theodora followed the progress of the building with pious zeal. Tradition tells that it caused her concern on more than one occasion. First, much had to be done to establish firm foundations under it; it was found that seepage from the Lycus River was weakening the subsoil. Then there was something even more disturbing. When they were about to begin the mosaic decorations, Theodora realized there would be a shortage of funds to carry on the work.

Happily, the apostles in whose honor the church was being built and whose remains were miraculously discovered under the ancient basilica, came to the empress's rescue.

She had a dream. Andrew, Luke, and Timothy appeared in it. "Do not be disturbed," they reassured her, "and do not ask your husband Justinian for the money. Go down to the seashore, near the Dexiocratus landing. There you will find twelve urns filled with gold pieces buried in the ground."

She obeyed them. At the spot they indicated the urns full of gold pieces were found. To prove the divine origin of their generosity, the coins were all impressed with the heads of the holy apostles. This was how the sovereign was able to complete the building and to endow it liberally.

Theodora never had the joy of seeing it entirely completed. It was not until two years after her death that the solemn dedication was celebrated on 28 June 550. The principal parts of the structure had been completed during her lifetime. Fulfilling Constantine's vow, she had installed in this Saint Denis of the Greek East, in an elaborate chapel, two magnificent marble sarcophagi for herself and her husband, in which later the golden coffins of the sovereigns were to repose.

In spite of her piety, her good works, her many benefactions, her zeal for all things religious, Theodora has been variously, and often harshly, judged by the church.

While some Eastern chroniclers call her "the saintly Theodora," and while her admirers in Syria proclaimed her constantly as "the empress who loves the Lord, who loves Christ, the ever faithful empress," and others praised her as "sustained by God himself in protecting the afflicted from the terrors of the tempest," other writers, especially those in the Latin West, could not denounce her enough with their insults and maledictions.

It was in the eyes of orthodox Catholics that Theodora was violently accused of heresy. She was openly a follower of the patriarch Severus and professed the Monophysite doctrine that rejected the creed of the Council of Chalcedon and accepted only one sole nature in the person of Jesus Christ.

To defend the friends of this doctrine, Theodora openly defied Rome. Until the day she died she resolutely protected its partisans against pontifical thunderbolts. As one historian says: "She revived the zeal of the heretics who were scattered through the empire; she encouraged those outside it with magnificent gifts."

This was not all. With her accustomed ardor, she tried to draw Justinian to the path she herself followed, and, in the best interests of the state itself, she tried to guide him toward a policy that obviously infuriated orthodox Catholics.

While the emperor's religious beliefs with respect to orthodoxy and his grandiose ambitions likewise inclined him toward maintaining union with Rome and toward persecuting dissenters, Theodora, less obedient and more farseeing, dreamed of other plans.

For twenty years, with her tenacious shrewdness, giving

way when expedient but surmounting all obstacles, Theodora pursued her aim and often succeeded in persuading her spouse against his will.

Death came to her too soon and prevented her from completing her task, but the religious policy she conceived does credit to her intelligence as a statesman. It supplies the measure of the influence she exercised over the whole spirit of Justinian's regime.

17

Politics and Theology

When Theodora mounted the throne of the Caesars with Justinian, a serious religious conflict had for a long time been troubling the whole of the Christian East. Since the fifth century subtle theologians had set themselves to try to explain how in Christ's person divinity and humanity were combined. The problem of the two natures and their unity profoundly agitated the church.

The Council of Chalcedon tried in vain, with the approval of Pope Leo the Great, to define orthodox doctrine on that issue, and to condemn with equal severity the heresy of Nestorius, which clearly distinguished two persons in Christ and that of Eutyches, which, on the contrary, admitted only one single nature in him.

The partisans of Eutyches, who called themselves Monophysites, and those of Nestorius equally refused to accept the condemnation. The Monophysite partisans in particular, led by men of great courage and supported by large popular majorities in Egypt and in Syria and by hordes of fanatical and indomitable monks, felt certain that some day the Monophysites would resume the leadership of the Byzantine church.

What augmented the gravity of what seemed to be only a theological controversy was that the eastern provinces of the empire, where the Monophysite doctrine was dominant, were attached to the Byzantine Empire by only the loosest ties of loyalty. In Egypt, in Syria, there were strongly developed nationalities, living their own lives, always ready to detach themselves from the monarchy. Their religious belief was hardly more than a form under which they manifested their separatist tendencies.

Furthermore, the emperors at the end of the fifth and the beginning of the sixth centuries, Zeno and Anastasius, made it their policy more to satisfy their Monophysite subjects by reasonable concessions in order to solidify the union with the Orient and, if necessary, even to sacrifice the union with Rome.

A different policy was introduced with the accession of Justin I, and especially with Justinian when Justinian brought his powerful and enduring tenacity to bear on church affairs. In face of the persecutions directed against them, Monophysites had been obliged to retreat. But, in spite of severities and exactions, the Monophysites remained powerful in Syria, in Palestine, in Armenia, in Mesopotamia, and above all in Egypt, where all the efforts of the orthodox remained ineffective. Everywhere in the Monophysite communities, much was expected of Theodora.

Since her youth, as we have seen, Theodora was in sympathy with Syrian and Egyptian Christianity. She preserved a tender and grateful recollection of her relations with it in that distant past. We know also that realistic political considerations inclined her to favor the eastern dissidents, and this increased the warmth of the sympathy she showed them. Even before coming to the throne she had actively applied her influence with Justinian in their favor, to try to temper the fury of the persecutions visited on them.

When she became empress she put her standing even more openly at their service. It was to her that heretic Egypt owed long years of tolerance, and to her that heretic Syria owed the revival of its persecuted national church. It was through her protection that the dissenters first were accepted and then permitted freely to resume their propaganda, and later were able to defy the ban of excommunication placed on them by the church councils, and the severities of the secular power. It was to her encouragement and her cooperation that the Monophysite missions owed their successes in Arabia, in Nubia, and in Abyssinia.

All her life she tried to find a middle ground for understanding and reconciliation to dissipate the resistance and appease the opposition of the Monophysite East and to reestablish peace both in the church and in the empire. It was not her fault if, in spite of Rome itself, the Monophysite doctrine did not become the universal dogma of the monarchy.

As a gift for the joy of her accession and a proof of her good intentions, Theodora began by inspiring the devout Justinian to an unexpected degree of toleration. Fugitive or proscribed bishops and monks were called back from exile and after long years of absence reentered their deserted and devastated churches and monasteries. At the empress's invitation Monophysites reappeared in Constantinople and even in the Sacred Palace. Against the stubborn opposition of the orthodox, they began to resume some standing at court.

Theodora did more for them. She persuaded Justinian to enter into direct negotiations with the dissenters. For a long time she had cherished great admiration for and a deep friendship with Severus, the deposed patriarch of Antioch, whom she had met long before at Alexandria. This distinguished prelate was one of the glories of the Monophysites because of his faith, his learning, his eloquence, and the steadfast courage he had shown under persecution. A lofty mind, conciliatory, an enemy of fruitless disputation, he seemed more capable than any other of lending himself to some form of accommodation.

The empress gave her husband to understand that, in spite of his repugnance, he ought to meet with so influential a personage. She succeeded in persuading him to believe that to make a conquest of such a man would result in countless agreements all through the Orient to approve the imperial policy.

The two sovereigns wrote very courteously to Severus

inviting him to come to Constantinople. But the patriarch, convinced that nothing would come of this tentative feeler, begged off and persisted in staying in Alexandria, assigning as his reasons his advanced age, his physical infirmity, and his white hairs.

This did not discourage Theodora. Lacking Severus, his disciples were asked to meet in conference with the orthodox "to reestablish unity," so the result was that a dialogue did take place at Constantinople.

The order of the day was, very characteristically, to show the dissenters perfect sweetness and unalterable patience. The imperial minister who conducted the proceedings spoke abundantly of "the paternal kindness that filled Justinian's heart." Justinian, who himself presided at the closing session, manifested outwardly a similar desire for conciliation.

In spite of the best of intentions, however, they could come to no understanding, much to Theodora's chagrin. But it was already a big point gained to be able to substitute so much good will for the previous rancor of persecution.

Meanwhile, thanks to the new policy of tolerance, the Monophysites regained much of the territory they had lost. In Asia, John of Tella, one of the most illustrious preachers of the sect, began an active propaganda in spite of the hesitation shown by other bishops in the sect. Again gathering around him small groups of the faithful, he taught them patiently, had them read the scriptures and sing psalms, and received them into the faith. For this he was denounced to the authorities and threatened with death, but he was not intimidated. He continued his meetings bravely, in secret and at night, gathering his followers around him. Shabbily clothed, using priestly symbols all broken, he made the same profound impression on his listeners as before. Always on the road, sometimes at Alexandria, sometimes in Constantinople, he made converts, ordained priests, and filled all Asia with missionaries. It is said that in a few years he brought into the Monophysite belief more than 176,000 persons.

In the capital, under the open protection of the empress, the dissenters were more active than ever before. The most illustrious theologians came into Constantinople, among them Peter the former bishop of Apamaeus, the monk Zooras, and many others. Severus himself, after much hesitation, finally agreed to go, in view of the empress's insistence and the reproaches of his coreligionists, who criticized his apparent inaction.

"Do not deceive yourselves," the holy man argued to them. "We shall not succeed in making a real peace treaty with this emperor. Nevertheless, I shall go up to Constantinople so as not to seem to block your hopes, but you will see that I shall return without having accomplished anything."

At first, events seemed to give the lie to his apprehensions. He was received by the emperor in great pomp, lodged at the palace at Theodora's invitation, and listened to with great respect by the sovereigns. He had an immediate and marked effect on religious affairs.

The Monophysites seemed actually to have conquered the capital. Confident of the empress's favor, they boldly declared war on the orthodox, pulpit against pulpit, baptistery against baptistery. In spite of official prohibition by law, they held assemblies, preached in churches and in private homes, in the town and in the outskirts, creating an uproar in the orthodox temples. As it was known the court thought well of them, their overt activities were not repressed.

Zooras edified all by his faith, his humility, and his charity in the monastery he built on the lot of ground given him by the empress. Every day the poor besieged his gates by the hundreds to share in the alms he distributed. Men of the world as well, senators and courtiers, were just as eager to assure him of their devotion, seeing how high he stood at the palace and how he was uttering opinions on the most serious of current issues.

Women especially were full of admiration for the Syrian preachers. The opponents of the Monophysites accused them of recruiting converts among courtesans, dancers, and lost women living a life of sin and luxury and adultery by the lightness of the penances they required and the ease with which they granted indulgences. Whatever the cause, their popularity among women was enormous.

Thanks also to hints they got from the court and the undisguised protection extended by certain highly placed personages at the palace, they made steady headway, especially in the higher levels of society. Hundreds of infants were brought to them to be baptized. Even in Justinian's immediate circle, there were chamberlains and senators who gloried in leading in their lives as laymen the rough existence of Syrian hermits.

In the hope of emulating the sainthood of the Syrians, Theodora's own grand chamberlain distributed his entire fortune in almsgiving and was happy to be reduced to poverty. Count Tribonius resigned from his offices at court, entered a retreat in a monastic cell, and spent his whole time divided between prayer and serving the unfortunate. Many connected with the palace tried to imitate these pious examples, hoping in this way both to earn the good will of their employers and to make certain of their eternal salvation.

Meanwhile, Epiphanius, patriarch of Constantinople, passed away. This produced another victory for the dissenters. There was a holy man, Anthimus, living in the monastery the empress had founded in the Hormisdas palace. He had formerly been the bishop of Trebizond. The Monophysites esteemed him highly for his theology, his way of life, his contempt for things of this world, and even more for the courage with which "he rose above the bonds of illusion and preached the true faith." Secretly he was allied with the cause of the heretics.

With Theodora's support he was elevated to the patriarchal throne. There he at once acknowledged the powerful influence of Severus and asked the advice of the man he considered one of the most learned theologians in the church.

At about the same time Timothy, patriarch of Alexandria, died. Theodora had been a strong admirer of this ardent defender of the Monophysite faith. She determined to provide a successor for him after her own heart. The army of fanatic monks gave its support to Gaianos, an uncompromising Monophysite. Theodora favored Theodosius, a more flexible and more manageable prelate. But the radicals were insisting on Gaianos, so she acted with vigor, in her usual way.

It was the custom at Alexandria that the successor of a patriarch stand watch at the bier of the deceased patriarch, lift the dead man's right hand, place it on his own head, and then, taking the scarf of Saint Mark off the deceased, place it around his own neck.

In spite of the official support he had from the authorities and the presence of an emissary from Theodora, the friends of Gaianos succeeded in preventing Theodosius from performing this ritual symbolizing the transfer of power. Troops were needed to install the empress's candidate. She sent a commissioner extraordinary, the eunuch Narses, her own chamberlain and obedient servant, to take command.

There was fighting in the streets for a few days. Even women took part in it from their house tops. Finally, as a last resort these houses were set on fire in order to suppress the rioting. At this point, the government controlled the weapons. Theodosius mounted the patriarchal throne.

Through Severus as an intermediary, Anthimus of Constantinople recognized the new bishop of Alexandria. With the high patronage of the empress and with the tacit approval of the emperor, the three patriarchs "in the interest of peace," as they put it, followed a line favorable to the Monophysites.

The opposing orthodox monks, as loyal guardians of the catholic faith, denounced in fiery letters the attitude and the progress made by the heretics. They called Severus a pagan serving demons and suspected of practicing magic, and Peter of Apamaeus they called a debauchee "serving only his own belly as God" and taking shameless and licentious liberties with women. They called Zooras a lunatic and Anthimus a hypocrite. All in vain. The emperor turned a deaf ear. To the great scandal of the catholics, the work of corruption, as they called it, continued to make horrifying progress.

Unfortunately for Theodora's plans, an unexpected adversary arrived in Constantinople at that moment. It was Pope Agapetus.

The king of the Goths had sent Pope Agapetus from Rome as an emissary to Justinian. He was received at court with a great show of honors. He opened the discussion of the religious problem but resolutely refused to have any communication with the heretic Anthimus. The emperor found it useless to try to persuade him. "Take my advice," the pope warned him, "or I'll send you into exile."

Theodora tried her best to win the pope over more subtly by promises of large payments, after failing to convince him by argument. But Agapetus was stiffened by the support of the whole body of orthodoxy. He would hear none of it.

Pressed from one side by his wife and from the other by the sovereign pontiff, the emperor was deeply embarrassed, until, if the legend can be trusted, God himself ruled openly in favor of the Monophysites.

In addition to demanding the removal of the patriarch, Agapetus insisted on the expulsion of Zooras. Justinian had given the pope an opportunity to see for himself that the monk was a violent character who feared no one. The pope required all the more forcefully that the Syrian be summoned to appear before him so he could force Zooras to submit to papal authority.

When the pope's messenger presented himself at the saint's monastery, he found the gates shut. Zooras sent word that it was the period of the Lenten fast so that divine law forbade his handling any business at such a time, no matter how important, even if it were for the emperor. "I have nothing more to say to you," he concluded. "If you wish to use force, that will be your affair." The nonplussed messenger returned to the palace.

The emperor was furious and sent the master of the offices himself with a detachment of guardsmen to arrest the saint. But just when the minister was embarking to cross the Golden Horn for the trip to the Sykae outskirts, a sudden gust of wind threw his boat back to the shore. He pushed off again, but just when he was to step ashore on the far bank, a huge sea monster rose up and shoved the vessel back into the middle of the stream with a terrific kick. The minister was extremely annoyed, swore roundly at the sailors, and ordered them back to their oars. Suddenly a thunderbolt struck the ship and demolished the bridge from stem to stern.

Then they understood that God himself was battling for Zooras. They fled with all possible speed. Justinian's messenger returned to take the news to the stupefied emperor.

But Providence failed to defend Anthimus with equal zeal. After resisting briefly, the emperor sacrificed Anthimus to the demands of the authorized representative of orthodoxy, Agapetus. The patriarch was deposed. Agapetus consecrated the priest Menas in his place.

It was a great success for the pope, but he got little joy of it. Less than a month later, he suddenly died. According to the customary practice, the catholics gave out that he had fallen a victim to magical incantations uttered by his opponents. The Monophysites rejoiced in his death as a just punishment by God, and, plucking up their courage, always with Theodora's support, they resumed their propaganda with fiery ardor.

At the Easter services Zooras was not afraid to baptize publicly a large number of infants brought to him by the best families at court. In their state of exaltation the dissenters went so far as openly to insult the emperor himself, whom they accused of having betrayed them. One fanatic, Isaac of Persia, dared to strike a statue of the emperor with his stick and crack its eyes. Excitement rose to a high pitch in the capital. It was feared the two factions would come to blows.

In this crisis Menas, the new patriarch, gave proof of his decisiveness. In May 531, in the Church of the Virgin, adjoining Saint Sophia, a council was assembled under his presidency to implement the decrees proclaimed by Agapetus. For several days a parade of heads and representatives of the orthodox monasteries in the capital, and of the holy communities in Syria, Palestine, and the Sinai, appeared before the assembled bishops. The holy fathers listened to a reading, with supporting evidence, of the charges brought by the stern guardians of the catholic faith denouncing Anthimus, Severus, Zooras, and Peter of Apamaeus to the pope and the emperor. Only the accused failed to respond.

The agents of the council looked for Anthimus all over Constantinople: in Saint Sophia; at the patriarchal palace; in churches where he might have taken refuge; at the Saint Sergius monastery, where it was suspected his supporters might have hidden him; even in the Sacred Palace and its oratory of Saint Michael Archangel, where he was said to have been seen.

Everywhere they found either closed gates or attendants ready to swear they had seen the patriarch recently but had no idea where he had gone. Considerably hindered by this, the emissaries went so far as to question even children in the streets for news of the disappearing defendant.

POLITICS AND THEOLOGY · 171

Theodora could have told the bishops where he was. At her hands Anthimus had found a secret and secure retreat right in the gynaeceum of the imperial palace itself. Through her protection, the other accused were likewise able to avoid being served.

This did not stop the council from taking action. It anathematized Anthimus, Severus, and Peter of Apamaeus in formal procedure, condemned their writings, declared them shorn of all ecclesiastical offices, and struck their names off the roll of the catholic church.

With this done and their work accomplished, the holy fathers, before adjourning, psalmodized the ritual acclamations: "Long live the emperor! Long live the patriarch! Anathema to Peter, Zooras, Severus, to the enemies of God! We have a Christian emperor; we have nothing to fear! Let us root out the lair of Zooras! Let us burn the dens of the heretics! Down with Peter's monasteries! We have an orthodox emperor; what have we to fear? Anathema to Severus, Peter, and Zooras! The Christian faith triumphant!"

Three months later Justinian returned completely to orthodoxy and obediently submitted to the will of the papal legate Pelagius. By an imperial decree he sanctioned the sentences pronounced by the council. Anthimus, Severus, and their partisans were forbidden to reside in Constantinople or any other large city of the Byzantine Empire. All persons were forbidden to harbor them or give them asylum under pain of confiscation.

Their books were proscribed. Making copies of them was prohibited under penalty of having one's hand cut off. They were forbidden to preach or to administer the sacraments of baptism or communion. This is how Justinian believed he was restoring peace in the Byzantine church and assuring the prosperity of the state.

Theodora had mistakenly ventured too far in estimating the power of her influence on the emperor. Her drive against orthodoxy and the pope broke down. It was all she could do to save her friends.

We know how she hid Anthimus. She also supplied Severus with the means of flight. The patriarch of Antioch was able to get away to Egypt to end there his long and laborious career in peace. Zooras was exiled to Thrace. Owing to the threatened resumption of the persecution, all that crowd of clerics, monks, and pastors who had tasted the hope of victory in Constantinople scattered in despair of their future with good reason.

In fact it was not long before there were fresh burnings at the stake in Syria, where monasteries were again closed down, before preachers were imprisoned or put to death, and the faithful Monophysite congregation reduced to misery under the energetic pressure applied by Ephraim, the orthodox patriarch of Antioch and his bishops, with the eager participation of the secular arm.

Egypt was also hit by the reaction. Patriarch Theodosius, the friend of Anthimus and Severus, was ordered to Constantinople, requested to resign, exiled to Thrace with his clergy, and replaced in Alexandria by a prelate capable of curbing all resistance—by terror if necessary. In a short time not more than three bishoprics occupied by the Monophysites survived in the whole Byzantine Empire.

Theodora was not a woman to be defeated by this setback. She had to bow under these circumstances and be present but powerless at the ruin of her friends and the triumph of the papacy, but, with her ever-daring and resilient talent, she began to plan her revenge.

While the Council of 536 was thundering its sterile anathemas, she took advantage of the death of Agapetus to plot to seat a pope of her choice on the pontifical throne. Under the influence of the papal legate Pelagius, Egypt, the last citadel of Monophysitism was, it is true, reduced to unimportance. Nevertheless, at Constantinople, right in the imperial palace itself, the empress patiently prepared to restore the persecuted Monophysite church.

18
Monks and Apostles

During the time that Monophysite monks, persecuted by the orthodox, were flowing into Constantinople from all over the East, Theodora, who was eager to offer them asylum and to show them some striking proof of her protection, made it a point to receive them openly at the Sacred Palace.

One of the cluster of buildings in the area of the imperial residence was the Hormizdas palace, on the shore of the Sea of Marmara. It had been Justinian's home while he was still the heir presumptive to the throne. When he rose to the throne he decided to preserve this home of his younger days. He had it magnificently restored. It was part of the complex within the enlarged palace grounds.

It was in this palace that Theodora decided to house her friends. She had no difficulty obtaining her husband's consent to this. Justinian was quite willing in this way to have the most notable leaders of the Monophysite opposition close at hand and under the surveillance of his own police.

Through the empress's efforts, then, the old Hormizdas palace was, as a contemporary wrote, converted "into a great and marvelous Desert of the Saints." The apartments were altered into cubicle cells. One of the large reception rooms was converted into a chapel, another into a refectory. In the courtyard and under the porticoes, wooden cabins roofed only with straw or rags were provided for the oldest and most illustrious of the religious, for those whose special sanctity was recognized, for anchorites and solitaries expelled from their hermitages, and for stylites forced to descend from their columns. In these they lived apart in meditation and prayer. The largest number of the brothers were assigned to a huge mansion, where they continued their cenobitic life under the direction of an abbot.

In this way there were more than five hundred monks assembled in one pious community, coming from a variety of countries, speaking a great variety of languages. All day long nothing was heard but the murmur of prayers and the psalmody of sacred hymns. Nothing was seen but old white-bearded monks prostrating themselves at the foot of altars, striving to earn their eternal salvation by austerity, fasting, and all-night supplication.

Soon the Syrians became noted all through the capital for their saintliness. First they were a cause for wonderment because of their intense devotion, but then they came to be admired for it. Thousands of the faithful came to the monastery eager to see the unusual sight or to receive benedictions from these saints. Even those obedient to the Council of Chalcedon were surprised and fascinated, sensing remorse and repentance gradually creeping into their hearts, so that many, touched by the virtue of the solitaries, were converted to the Monophysite doctrine.

Theodora, in her ardor, was a constant visitor to her wards. She went to kneel at the feet of the cenobites every two or three days, asking their benedictions and begging them to pray for her, and bringing them generous gifts as alms. Finally she even persuaded Justinian to accompany her in spite of his previous objections. He, too, filled with admiration, felt so profoundly moved by the conversations he had with the monks that he was willing, like his wife, to honor and protect them.

Needless to say, this general enthusiasm was nourished by miracles that were soon reported and that further enhanced the reputation in Byzantium of the pious community. One day a throng of the faithful crowded forward in the chapel in great numbers to receive communion. As usual there were many women and children among them. Suddenly, with a great crash, the building collapsed under their weight, engulfing hundreds of victims. Moans, shrieks of terror, and sorrow rose from every side. The sound was heard as far away as the Sacred Palace. Soon the news of the terrible catastrophe spread over the whole city.

But God in his mercy watched over his chosen. After a brief moment of stupefaction, all who were present rose up unharmed, without a single wound or bruise, praising and singing to the Lord, who had saved them from certain death. This striking miracle made the sovereigns, all the mighty and the whole city, pay even more honor to the sainted inhabitants of the monastery. Justinian himself paid them the tribute of rebuilding the collapsed structure at his own cost.

During the difficult years following the Council of 536, while persecution was raging all through the empire, the Monophysite monastery of Saint Sergius, the name under which the monastery at the Hormizdas palace was consecrated, escaped the fury of the tempest owing to the empress's protection. Actually, the monks in it were, in a way, prisoners in their own retreat. To move away from the capital or even to take a trip outside the city, they had to get a government permit. Yet they exercised considerable influence on all around them, and while, it is true, the number of their cenobites was gradually diminishing, some of them having obtained permission to return to their native countries, the monastery prospered as long as Theodora lived. Even after her death, Justinian continued to protect it as a tribute to her memory.

About the same time, another Monophysite community maintained itself within the gates of the capital, also with the empress's support. This was the Syrian monastery, on the eastern shore of the Golden Horn, in the Sykae outskirts opposite the church and palace of Saint Mamas. It had been established on the plot of ground Theodora presented to the monk Zooras. Many of the dissenters who came to the capital found peace and security in it.

On a neighboring tract the pious Maras had laid out a cemetery for his coreligionists. A large number of illustrious communicants of the sect had been buried in this consecrated ground. Its monastery had been a holy gathering place for Monophysites, and it flourished. Its head, the abbot John, a monk from Amida in Mesopotamia, was very highly regarded by the empress and even by the emperor. The latter, impressed by the abbot's zeal in denouncing paganism, agreed to overlook his heretical beliefs.

All the notables of the sect gradually made it their practice to gather in that safe retreat so that it became a center for its propaganda and its decisions.

That was how Theodora protected her friends in spite of the formal edicts, the legal prohibitions, and the fury of the persecution. She set up refuges for Monophysites everywhere. She founded a house of refuge for expelled bishops and proscribed monks alongside the tomb of the holy martyr Isidore on the Island of Chios. At Derkos, on the Black Sea, she spared no effort to ameliorate the semicaptivity of her partisans, who were expected to include the monk Zooras if he were exiled at the time of the crisis of 536, and then the patriarch Theodosius and his clergy.

Not content merely to subsidize their needs liberally, Theodora discreetly encouraged their propaganda and arranged for many of the faithful to have access to their pastors when they were in need of consolation and aid. Most of all, she placed at their disposal the means for making an early return to the capital, so they might then gather around her and reorganize all the sect's forces.

The eastern populations persisted in their beliefs in spite of the death or exile of their priests. At the same time, the principal leaders of the sect understood very clearly that the restoration of their church could be accomplished only if the palace made it possible. They knew they had to con-

centrate their efforts on Constantinople, in order, according to the phrase of the chronicler, "to soften up the emperor and keep the zeal of the empress kindled for the faithful."

These were the policies they planned to follow. For the time being they must hold themselves prudently in reserve. They pretended to respect the government's orders, not showing themselves too active in propaganda or the ordaining of new priests. They relied on time and on Theodora.

This devious attitude, however, did not satisfy all their coreligionists. There were fanatics and enthusiasts among the Monophysites who caused the empress plenty of worry.

John, formerly bishop of Memphis in Egypt, was one of the most impatient in this irreconcilable group in the sect. He had followed the patriarch Theodosius into exile, but his emotional and energetic spirit, thirsting for a martyr's glory, found the quiet life he had to lead at Derkos not at all to his taste but too prudent and dull. He was ready to change it.

He would complain: "They call us the pastors of the church, yet they let the wolves fall upon our lambs. We stay quietly at home when we should be out dying for our faith."

It made John sad to see about him bishops who, only out of fear of the government, refused the consolations of religion to the faithful who came to them from far away. "By the living God," he would grumble, "I cannot see what stops me from going to the great church or to the forum in the capital and performing my religious duties in the presence of the whole world."

At last, under the pretext of being ill, John received permission to go up to Constantinople to get medical treatment. He was very well received by the empress, who saw to his lodging and maintenance herself. He soon began to preach freely, setting up his altars and instructing the faithful.

The more politic leaders of the sect, disturbed by his intemperate zeal, warned him that he was throwing himself

"into the lion's jaws" and that he was gravely compromising the sect itself by his mad impetuousness. But the Egyptian would hear none of this. He declared with contempt that the word of God would keep the lion's jaws open. The leaders asked the patriarch to recall him to Derkos.

But Theodosius, who was secretly delighted with his disciple's recalcitrancy, kept out of the quarrel, explaining that the empress was well informed of John's intentions and had given him a favorable reception.

So they went back to Theodora. The Monophysite bishops begged her to send the Egyptian away from the capital. Thinking this would satisfy her friends, she willingly agreed. But when word came to John in her name to leave at once under pain of death, he ran straight to the palace with his customary courage. When he got in to see the sovereign, he began at once to rebuke her violently for agreeing with Justinian to sadden God and his church. Theodora could not understand him. He retorted: "But was it not you who ordered me to leave the city? Did you not threaten me with death? What advantage would this be to you?"

He was told that the empress was very distressed at her disobedient followers and would not forgive them for this breach of her instructions unless John himself would petition her for pardon. At the same time she tried to calm down his excessive zeal somewhat. "Be warned," she advised him, "to stay here in the palace for fear some misfortune might happen to you. Behave quietly, as your comrades are doing. Stop ordaining priests here in the capital."

John was discriminating. He understood that there can be pious falsehoods. He agreed: "I have no wish to do so. I came here only with the intent of asking your permission to spend thirty or forty days quietly in a house in the country because I am a sick man." Theodora was pleased and gave him the permission he asked.

But John used her permission to go off to preach in Asia Minor. Disguised as a beggar, he got as far as Tarsus, meet-

ing with great success wherever he went. Consequently the orthodox were increasingly annoyed by his activities. Their bishops sent Justinian very urgent letters informing him that a heretic bishop had escaped from the capital and was making trouble all over the country. This time again John slipped out of the noose by his dexterity.

He returned in great haste to Byzantium. There he wrote at once to Theodora that he regretted that he had not been able to go to see her for such a long time because his poor health had made it impossible for him to leave his retreat. Then, when the public inquiry that was instituted seemed to point to John as the culprit bishop, Theodora herself gave assurance that the saint had never left the house in the country to which she had given him permission to retire. When his accusers went there to inspect it, they actually found him there, to their immediate embarrassment.

Several times John succeeded in resuming his evangelical conversions by ingenious devices of this sort. Forewarned of his route, the faithful would assemble in great secrecy at the indicated meeting place at night. While sentries watched over the security of the assemblage, the bishop gave communion, ordained priests, and gave the faithful courage. By the time the orthodox would learn of his arrival, he had already left. His work in the capital was no less active. The Monophysite leaders ended by bowing to his indomitable courage and indefatigable zeal.

Meantime, they, too, carried on their labors by other means. Thanks to the empress, Theodosius and his friends had been recalled to Constantinople, and soon the former patriarch's house became the headquarters of the sect. All the active and energetic leaders met there. Besides old fighters like Zooras and Peter of Apamaeus, there were men such as Julian, the future apostle of Nubia; Theodore, the future bishop of Arabia; Sergius of Tella, the future patriarch of Antioch; Sergius's friend Jacob Baradaeus, who was later to occupy the see of Edessa and revive the Monophysite church;

and still others such as John, abbot of the Syrian monastery later to become bishop of Ephesus, and Constantine, who had been bishop of Laodicea.

They were openly protected by Theodora, who had long known most of them. They were well received at court. The empress constantly commended them to the emperor and frequently urged them on him. Once again the orthodox Christians complained that the Monophysites were perfidiously contaminating the palace and a large section of the population of the capital.

Soon they were doing even more. The orthodox persecution had swept most of the dissident bishops out of their episcopal sees and the government was watching carefully to stop the recruitment of more schismatic clergy. Therefore what the Monophysites had to do above all was to create additional leaders for the faithful. In spite of all the precautions taken against them, they succeeded with the complicity of the empress.

The opportunity to do so came in 543. Harith, the Syrian Ghassanid, who was prince of the Arab tribes in the Syrian desert, asked Theodora to send him several bishops to induct his subjects into the Christian faith. She looked around eagerly to select priests among her Monophysite friends, and, what is even more remarkable, she got Justinian to approve her choices.

He was glad to have some of the dissident clergy, who in any case were causing him much embarrassment in the capital, go away on foreign missions and use up the energy that was devouring these schismatic preachers. He had already made use of them to convert the Arabs in the Yemen, the Abyssinians in the kingdom of Aksoum, and to bring into the Christian faith the pagans of Nubia and of the Blemmyian country. We have already described how Theodora had endorsed that mission with all her powers. So the two sovereigns were at one in choosing bishops of the Monophysite persuasion to answer the call from the desert prince.

For about fifteen years the monk from Tella, Jacob

Baradaeus, had been living in Constantinople. He was a very learned man, brought up on both Syrian and Greek, even more celebrated for his fasting, his austerities, the simplicity of his life, and his exceeding modesty. When quite young he had taken a vow of poverty and distributed his entire fortune to the needy. He early became famous for the carelessness of his dress, the roughness of his manners, and the miraculous cures he worked.

Jacob came to the capital late and was well received by the empress. He considered it wiser to withdraw from the dangers of the world. He shut himself up in a narrow cell, wished to see no one, never spoke to anyone, and was all the more admired by all.

Harith the Ghassanid held him in particularly high esteem after meeting him and having evidence of his prophetic clairvoyance. Theodora, who knew him well, had a real feeling of admiration for him. It was this meditative solitary and ascetic that she selected to send to convert the Arabs and restore the Monophysite church. Events proved she had made no mistake.

Acting on her advice, Theodosius appointed Jacob to the see of Edessa and another monk in his own group, the Arab Theodore, to the see of Bostra. In spite of their dislike for doing so, both had to accede to Theodora's official command and return to the active life they had hoped to leave behind them. They left for their dioceses after being consecrated by Theodosius, the former patriarch of Alexandria.

In addition to their official mission both apostles were given secret instructions. With the acquiescence of Theodora, the patriarch authorized them to ordain priests, create bishops, and, in short, to restore the Monophysite clergy of the Orient in the whole area under their jurisdiction. In addition, beyond the narrow limits of their actual dioceses, he assigned all of Arabia, Palestine, and the desert to Theodore, and the whole of Syria and Asia Minor to Jacob Baradaeus.

The empress agreed with Theodosius. She encouraged

this organization of propaganda and promised to exert her influence in aid of the two prelates.

In a few years Jacob Baradaeus, by his energy, his zeal, and his courage, had truly restored the Monophysite church. He resumed the labors that first John of Tella and later John the Egyptian, had initiated in the Asian provinces. Frequently concealing himself in the habit of a mendicant friar, he traveled all through Syria, Armenia, Cappadocia, Cilicia, Isauria, Pamphylia, Asia Minor, and the islands of Rhodes, Cyprus, Chios, and Mytilene, preaching and giving instructions, ordaining priests for new religious communities, organizing dioceses, and appointing bishops.

As the chronicler reports: "He made priesthood spread all through the Byzantine Empire like a great river." Orthodox priests, alarmed at the turmoil the apostle aroused, tried without success to have Jacob arrested. Justinian put a price on his head but to no effect. The saint outmanoeuvred all the schemes of his persecutors and continued forward "on the path of justice." Always on foot, leading an ascetic life everywhere, he was now in Constantinople, now in Asia, now in Alexandria, always tireless, always unappeasable.

His friends were sure that God himself protected Jacob and beclouded the wits of his enemies. In Monophysite circles the story was told, with some zest, that on one occasion the government horsemen stopped him to ask: "Have you not heard tell that Jacob the impostor has been in such-and-such a place?" and that, in jest, Jacob answered: "Yes, I believe I have heard he is circulating in that district." Then, pointing to a direction just the opposite to that he intended to take, he said, "So, if you push your horses hard, you will positively catch up with him."

Theodora's friendship and the shrewdness of Jacob's coreligionists in the capital protected him even more securely.

Canon law required the presence of three bishops to make the consecration of a new bishop valid. On the advice of the patriarch Theodosius, Jacob began his campaign by proceeding first to Alexandria. There he had no difficulty in finding three prelates who, by order of their former metropolitan, joined in conferring the episcopate on two of his disciples. With their cooperation, Jacob in his turn ordained additional bishops in the principal cities of Syria and Asia.

At the same time the prelates who stayed in Constantinople consecrated twelve bishops for Egypt and the Thebaid, and, to fill the vacancy caused by the death of Severus in the patriarchate of Antioch, they appointed the wise and pious Sergius of Tella, a friend of Jacob.

In this way an entire nongovernmental episcopate was set up to direct the newly revived Monophysite church, which kept the name of Jacobite in honor of its great founder.

Beyond that, to strengthen the action of her dependents, Theodora very craftily contrived to manage appointments for some of them from the government itself. In this way John, who was secretly appointed the Monophysite bishop of Ephesus, was sent by Justinian to Caria, Lydia, and Phrygia to combat paganism there. He performed that duty conscientiously, earning the title of "destroyer of idols and the hammer on the pagans." But he rendered even greater service to his sect and covered his diocese with Monophysite churches and monasteries.

In a few years the products of Jacob Baradaeus's apostolate included two patriarchs, twenty-seven consecrated bishops, and more than a hundred thousand ordained priests and deacons. His faith performed miracles. He exorcised demons, brought the dead back to life, and predicted the future. His faith spread "like a delicate perfume" all over the world, well beyond the boundaries of the Byzantine Empire.

Thanks to his activity, most of the Orient returned to the faith that all were justified in calling "the faith of Saints Jacob and Theodosius." Even outside the monarchy, in

Persia, Arabia, Abyssinia, and Nubia, powerful churches accepted the Monophysite belief.

Theodora could be proud of what she had accomplished, after having so long been the protectress of Christians in distant lands and having all her life labored for the triumph of Monophysitism.

The obscure monk she had once seen in a dream refreshing the Roman people with running water, the pious solitary whom she had long before received at Constantinople and in whom she had put so much faith, had largely fulfilled her hopes.

By the time Theodora died, having seen the growing success of Jacob's apostolate, she could well believe that the dream of her religious policy had been realized. If even today the Jacobite church exists in Egypt and in Syria, the glory belongs largely to Jacob Baradaeus and to Theodora.

19
Empress and Pope

When Pope Agapetus suddenly died in Constantinople in 536, Theodora conceived an audacious plan to profit by the unexpected vacancy created in the pontifical see.

For some years the deacon Vigilius had been living at Constantinople as the papal nuncio. He was ambitious, without scruples, capable of making good use of the weaknesses of others and of striking a good bargain. Born of a great senatorial family, he had already once before tried to mount Saint Peter's throne. To that end he had gotten Saint Boniface II to adopt him as successor. He was obliged to abandon that hope, however, owing to opposition that developed among the clergy in Rome. He then turned toward the Byzantines. He used his diplomatic status shrewdly to advance himself in Theodora's favor.

When the empress, furious at having to bow to Agapetus's demands, dreamed of having her revenge by making pope a man of her own choice who would be ready to come to terms with the Monophysites, Vigilius, with his high standing at her court, seemed to her the man she needed to serve her purpose. His ambition seemed to assure his readiness to make a deal. He and she had no difficulty in understanding each other. The empress offered him the succession to Agapetus. He promised that, once on the pontifical throne, he would willingly be the completely pliant instrument to carry out her wishes. It is said that, in addition, he later bound himself to her more specifically: he promised that in exchange for Byzantine support he would renounce the decrees of Chalcedon, reinstate Anthimus, and write to Theodosius and Severus, the great leaders of Mono-physitism, to assure them of his complete conformity with their views. It is also said that, as the price of these services expected of him, Theodora paid him a large sum of money.

A most penetrating historian later wrote of this trans-action: "Anyone who had studied the character of Vigilius knew that any deal he would make might be set aside by him for cash. He would promise anything, or at least lead one to believe that he could hope for it."

What is certain is that he left for Rome in great haste, carrying letters to Belisarius and Antonina, and that these letters outlined in unmistakable terms the duty expected of the general. Obviously, Justinian had given Theodora a free hand as to the nomination of a candidate to the papacy in order to compensate her for the setback she had just expe-rienced, and perhaps also secretly hoping for a solution that might reestablish peace in the Byzantine church by seating a Roman pontiff willing to strike an accord with the Oriental church.

While this deal was being negotiated in Constanti-nople, events were marching on in the Eternal City. Al-though at that date Belisarius had already landed on the Italian coast, Rome itself was still in the hands of the Goths. Their king, Theodatus, sensed by instinct how important it would be for him at this juncture to assure himself of his own pope. In all haste he gave the deacon Silverius assur-ance of his support and had him nominated as Agapetus's successor, sure that the deacon was devoted to his interests.

When Vigilius arrived in Italy, the throne of Saint Peter he aimed at was already occupied. It would be nec-essary first to have Silverius step down from it before he could take the seat in accordance with his deal with Theo-dora. One very serious and troublesome obstacle to this was that the new pontiff, to make himself acceptable at Constan-tinople, had made it his first order of business to call for the entry of imperial troops into Rome. He actually surrendered it to Belisarius in December 536.

Vigilius was completely frustrated. Theodora was even more annoyed. As personalities were basically of little concern to her, however, she tried to get from Silverius what she had hoped to get from Vigilius. She sent him her request that he reseat Anthimus on the patriarchal throne. The pontiff vigorously refused. This made her decide to act against him with equal vigor.

Official orders were sent to Belisarius enjoining him to depose Silverius and elevate Vigilius to his place. The patrician hesitated, much embarrassed by the distasteful task imposed on him. But Antonina, always close to him and also most anxious to please Theodora, beat his scruples down. Vigilius, too, organized support around the general to stimulate his success. It is said he employed equally convincing arguments by promising Belisarius money. As it was risky in any event for the general to thwart the empress's wishes, Belisarius wound up by lending himself to a conspiracy being woven against the unfortunate Silverius.

At that moment the Ostrogoths, under orders of their king, Vitigis, had just taken the offensive again. A formidable army was laying siege to Rome. To defend Rome, Belisarius had barely five thousand men, entrenched behind walls in bad repair, surrounded by a discontented population that was restless at being compelled to sustain the horrors of a siege. There was suspicion that the winds of treason would blow over it.

For this reason, when letters were brought to the general, supposedly written by the pope and offering to surrender the Asinaria Gate close by the Lateran palace, where the pope lived, Belisarius, though he was furious at first, soon realized that these supposed proofs of betrayal had been shamelessly forged. He was touched by sympathy for the victim. He tried secretly, with Antonina's knowledge, to make one last effort on behalf of Silverius.

He hinted to Silverius that Silverius himself should offer Theodora the concessions she had hoped to obtain through the good will of Vigilius, and in this way avoid the fate that was threatening him. Silverius, conscious that he was the guardian of orthodoxy, courageously refused. Events then had to run their course.

To refute the rumors of treason that were circulating against him, Silverius left the Lateran and moved far away from the city walls to the Church of Saint Sabina. It was there that Belisarius sent to find him, promising him through his stepson, Photius, that no untimely harm would come to him.

In spite of the fears of his attendants, who distrusted Greek oaths, Silverius went to the Pincio palace of Belisarius. His first interview there ended peaceably, although at the last moment Belisarius was uncertain what to do.

A few days later the pope was again asked to go to see the general. This time the pontiff was uneasy and at first declined to leave the church that was his refuge. Finally he decided to go. He went accompanied by a numerous group of attendants, entrusting his cause to God.

As soon as Silverius arrived at the palace, he was separated from his companions. They were told to wait in the antechambers. He was left alone with Vigilius. They were escorted into the private apartments. There a strange spectacle awaited them. Antonina lay negligently on her couch, like a sovereign receiving a subject. Belisarius was amorously seated at her feet like a servitor obedient to all her wishes.

"Ah, well, my Lord Pope," began Belisarius's wife. "What have we done to you, we Romans, to make you want to deliver us over to the Goths?" We do not know what more was said, but we do know what was done. The pope was stripped of all his insignia of office and reclothed in a monk's habit. Then a servant of the general went out to the antechamber and announced to the waiting clerics: "My Lord

Pope has been deposed and made a monk." In the general consternation that ensued, Vigilius was elected pope the next day, under pressure from the Byzantine authorities. That was 29 March 537.

The unhappy Silverius was sent into Lycia by Belisarius, never again to see the Eternal City. For a brief moment Justinian, who was shocked by the enormity of the crime perpetrated against the pontiff, thought of insisting on a regular trial and restoring Silverius to his throne if he were found innocent. In spite of Theodora, Justinian ordered that Silverius be brought back to Rome. Vigilius was much disturbed and demanded to be told what was going to happen.

Fortunately, Antonina was there. Always anxious to please the empress, she persuaded Belisarius to deliver the unfortunate predecessor to the emissaries of Vigilius. Silverius was banished to the island of Palmaria, reduced to "the bread of sorrow and the water of anguish," and died soon after, the innocent victim of the ambition of Vigilius, the schemes of Antonina, and the policy of Theodora.

The empress thought she had at last succeeded. She had made a pope obedient to her will. But, once in office, Vigilius changed his attitude. In spite of Antonina's advice and a summons from Belisarius, he tried to evade the performance and modify the terms of what he had promised. His enemies, it is true, charge that he ended by giving in and that he wrote to the great leaders of Monophysitism, Theodosius, Anthimus, and Severus, agreeing to adhere completely to their doctrine. But the authenticity of this document is under suspicion, while the official professions of faith that the pope addressed to the emperor and to patriarch Menas are, on the contrary, severely orthodox.

In fact, circumstances developed that supplied Vigilius with the excuses he wanted to avoid having to carry out the pledges he had given. Italy had been devastated by the war. Its situation was so critical that no pope could be criticized if he set aside doctrinal controversy for the time being. In addition, the loyalty, which was widespread in the West, to the Council of Chalcedon and the tradition of Saint Leo justified the caution the pontiff exercised.

Theodora herself seems to have realized the danger inherent in pushing her plans too ruthlessly. Confident that she had a pledge from Vigilius, she waited, though at first impatiently, for the propitious moment to come when he could fulfill his commitments to her. As to Justinian, who was then very responsive to the influence of the papal nuncio Pelagius, a great friend of the pope, he basically had no strong wish to favor the Monophysites. This all made it possible for Vigilius to remain true to Roman orthodoxy without becoming embroiled with Theodora. The result was that, in spite of the empress's plotting, her attempt to lay rough hands on the apostolic see ran completely aground.

But she was not by any means a woman who could be frustrated with impunity. She proved that again on this occasion.

She had once made use of a dubious character named Arsenius, an adherent of the heretic sect of Samaritans. She had in return made him rich, a senator, and well known. When the Samaritans revolted in Palestine, she willingly adopted suggestions he made against the Christians. But since then he had changed sides and been converted to orthodox Christianity. Baptized by Saint Sabas, Arsenius defended his new beliefs with all the zeal of a convert. He had retired to Alexandria where he tried to please the emperor by favoring all the forces of Chalcedonian reaction that had, with government support, installed the patriarch Paul as successor to Theodosius.

Theodora naturally held this defection against Arsenius, and she let him know it. The Monophysite opposition in Egypt was gradually growing stronger and the orthodox patriarch was imposing ever more severe penalties accordingly. Arsenius was overzealous. He got Rhodon, the imperial prefect, to execute one of the metropolitan's opponents without the formality of a trial. This was illegal, and the refinements of cruelty that accompanied the execution increased its horror.

The empress seized on this episode with great satisfaction. Arsenius and Rhodon were arrested, tried, and executed. Their possessions were confiscated. Patriarch Paul, in spite of his denials, was implicated in the affair as an accomplice and deposed by the Synod of Gaza. The empress could be proud of her work. At one stroke she did away with a prelate hateful to the Monophysites, she gave a stunning example of how risky it was for bureaucrats to serve the interests of the orthodox too obediently—even on orders from the emperor—and she punished a former friend who had turned traitor on her. Vigilius also got a demonstration of the tenacity of her hate and of how unwise it would be for him to deceive her hopes.

That was at the time the Monophysite church, with help from the empress, had begun to revive. The official prelates at court had begun to search for a common ground on which to stand with the dissidents, to please the sovereign. One of them, Theodore Askidas, bishop of Caesarea, had the good fortune to identify three small sections in the text approved by the Council of Chalcedon, the "Three Chapters" as they came to be called, obviously tainted by the Nestorian heresy, the authors of which were deeply odious to the Monophysites.

Askidas was much gratified to have made this discovery. With it he hoped to steal a march on the papal nuncio Pelagius, his rival for influence at court. He told Justinian what he had found, and he flattered the emperor's pride in his theological learning by asking him to study the issue. He also argued to Justinian that this would provide a platform, both convenient and orthodox, for dispelling the distrust of the Monophysites because from it a Chalcedon creed, "now purified and renewed," could be accepted by all sides without difficulty.

Justinian, under Theodora's influence, was still dreaming of a policy of conciliation and let himself be persuaded. The Monophysite dissidents, even the most intransigent of them, were delighted to see the work of Saint Leo being called into question. They pressed for the adoption of the new formula for union. The battle of the "Three Chapters" had begun. This is when Theodora came back at Vigilius. The pope was asked to give his sanction to the edict by which the emperor condemned the incriminating text. To speed his approval, Justinian applied brute force.

On 22 November 545, when the pope was celebrating mass in the basilica of Saint Cecilia in Trastevere, the church was suddenly surrounded by soldiers. The imperial secretary in command of the detachment entered the sanctuary and motioned to the pontiff to follow him at once. Before those present realized what was happening, Vigilius was arrested and promptly put aboard a ship moored close by in the Tiber. While this was being done, a crowd was gathering on the shore. The faithful who had followed the pope were uttering groans and begging his blessing in loud cries. Vigilius pronounced the benediction over them from the ship's bridge and the shipside congregation piously responded "Amen."

The imperial agent got the vessel under way, and it began to descend the stream. Then there was another outburst. In the multitude there were also many who detested the pontiff. They began to jeer him while a hail of sticks, stones, and other missiles rained down on the ship. "Death to you!" this crowd shouted. "Bad luck to you! You have done us Romans harm! May you have harm done you wherever you go!" At last the ship, driven along by the current, passed out of range of these ill-wishers. Vigilius reached Porto and from there reembarked for Syracuse.

Popular imagination attributed this theatrical stroke to Theodora. It was rumored that it was she who ordered this abduction by writing to her emissary: "Arrest Vigilius wher-

ever you can find him except in the basilica of Saint Peter's
and bring him to us. If you do not, then, by the living God,
I will have you flayed alive."

Whatever basis there may have been for this gossip, it
is very likely that the pope, doubtlessly in fear of vengeance
from the sovereign whose hopes he had betrayed, and being
unwilling to step into the hornet's nest of the "Three Chapters," lost no time in finding his way back to Constantinople.
It took him three months to make the journey from Syracuse
to Constantinople, finally arriving there on 25 January 547.
This gave him plenty of leisure to think things over and to
revive his courage. As he now felt confident that he would
be supported by the opposition of the whole Occident to the
wishes of Theodora, he brought with him sentiments quite
other than those the court expected.

Just as Agapetus did before with regard to Anthimus,
Vigilius refused to meet with patriarch Menas but brutally
excommunicated him and his followers.

Then, embarrassed by his recollection of the commitments he had previously made, bowing to the obsession of
the emperor for unity and to the energetic determination
of Theodora, and also flattered by the courtesies being showered on him by the Byzantine court theologians, he began to
weaken and to consider the possibility of anathematizing the
"Three Chapters." After June came, Vigilius made up with
Menas to please the empress.

A little later he took still a further step. It was demonstrated to him that he could condemn the "Three Chapters"
without touching the rest of the council's conclusions. Now
he was not so certain of his previous position. But he stood
firm, even in the face of threats, in stubbornly refusing to
subscribe to the imperial edict on the ground that the successor of Saint Peter could never bind himself merely to
ratify the decisions of an emperor in matters concerning the
faith. Yet he did commit himself formally, in the presence
of the emperor and his cabinet, to condemning the "Three

Chapters," and, as a pledge of good faith, he sent Justinian and Theodora an express declaration to this effect with his signature.

On the eve of Easter 548 Vigilius promulgated his decree, proud of having been able to resolve the difficulty of the situation, enthusiastic at the thought that he had settled so violent a controversy, and flattered that by his vision he had restored peace to the church. He roughly closed the mouths of those of his staff who objected to this decision. He formally preserved the authority of the Council of Chalcedon but equally clearly condemned the authors and the text of the three suspected paragraphs.

This was Theodora's last victory. On the eve of her death, seeing the pope's humiliation accomplished and the growing progress of the Monophysite church, she could believe she had avenged her defeat of 536, punished Vigilius for the deception he had practiced on her, and, by her tenacious energy, brought to fruition the success of the religious policy of which she had dreamed.

The Western church has never forgiven Theodora—for her brutal deposition of Silverius, for the stubborn fidelity with which she adhered to Monophysitism, or for the dictatorial authority with which she indulged her hatred of ecclesiastical personages, of which Vigilius in particular had such bitter experience. With self-satisfied animus it has even charged her with all sorts of offenses, beyond those that we are sure, in all good conscience, she could not be held responsible for, on the principle of the old maxim that you lend only to the rich. Among these charged offenses is the harsh treatment accorded Vigilius, that certainly took place incontestably only after her death.

From century to century, ecclesiastic historians have heaped insults and maledictions on Theodora's name. There is something almost ridiculous in the venom with which some of them denounce in Justinian's wife "a second Eve, too susceptible to the serpent, a new Delilah, another

Herodias quenching her thirst with the blood of saints, a citizen of hell moved by the spirit of Satan, prodded by the devil's prong, driven relentlessly to violate the harmony bought by the blood of saints and martyrs."

Theodora deserves to be judged otherwise than by this flood of vitriolic words. There is no doubt that, to further her designs, she applied more fiery ardor, more dictatorial violence, more obstinate and implacable hatred, sometimes more icy cruelty, than was called for. Yet she also brought to what she did eminent qualities of ability, virile firmness, a very real understanding of the necessities of government, clear intelligence, and statesmanlike strength of a high order.

Theodora was undeviating in her aspirations and loyal to her friends. The complex policy that she persuaded Justinian to follow in the field of religion was, in spite of his hesitancies and his retreats, when all is said and done, in every way worthy of an emperor.

20

Theodora's Death

After a long illness Theodora died of cancer 29 June 548. To pay the deceased empress their respects for the last time a gathering of courtiers and dignitaries assembled around her in the great hall of the palace. In accordance with the prescribed ceremonial, the embalmed body of the sovereign lay in state in the triclinium of nineteen couches.

Her body reposed on the golden state bier clad in the purple, her head crowned with the diadem, her feet shod in the purple buskins. Death had not yet left its mark on the beautiful features that were exposed. Only a little paler than usual, she seemed only to be sleeping peacefully.

The most precious crown jewels sparkled around the high catafalque. Hundreds of gold and silver torches, fixed on columns, burned fitfully. The vapors of Arabian incense and the sweetish odors of balsam rose in the heavy air among the flames of myriad tapers. Eunuchs, cubiculars, and the ladies-in-waiting of the imperial household wept sadly at the foot of the funeral couch.

One last time all Constantinople passed the dead sovereign in review in solemn procession. Patriarch Menas, followed by the numerous clergy of the great church; Pope Vigilius accompanied by his bishops and monks; then the senate in formal uniforms, the patricians, the magistrates, the high military commanders, the throng of court and government dignitaries; then a long line of women, the wives of patricians, magistrates, and prefects, of consuls, quaestors, and excubitors; then the ladies-in-waiting and the servants of the residence; at the call of the grand marshal all came forward in succession to do the dead empress their last homage.

At the end of the long procession came the princes of the imperial family. Finally, Justinian himself came forward, weeping bitterly, crushed by the weight of the irreparable loss he had suffered. He brought the woman he had adored, as a last and supreme gift and remembrance, lavish jewels, magnificent materials embroidered in gold and sparkling with gems, all the funereal ornament that must go with her into the tomb as a last evidence of the luxury and the pomp she had loved so dearly in life. Taking the loved inanimate body in his arms, the old emperor, his eyes streaming with tears, murmured his last farewell to his Theodora.

Then, at his gesture, the imperial bearers lifted the funeral couch. The grand master of ceremonies, approaching the corpse, intoned the ritual words three times in a loud voice: "Go, Empress, from us. The King of Kings, the Sovereign of all Sovereigns, calls thee." Then, following the coffin, the imperial procession formed and passed for a last time through the vaulted passages of the palace.

Outside, under the porticoes of the Augusteum, the crowd awaited the passage of the procession. At the doors, on the terraces, from the windows of houses, women with their hair all disheveled, wept silently or uttered piercing cries. In the streets beflagged with banners, strewn with gilded sand, the incense rose in thick clouds while the procession advanced in pomp and magnificence through throngs of people drawn by the grandeur of the spectacle.

The sacred chanting of the priests and the psalms of the maidens mingled with the sounds of mourning, the pealing of the silver organs, and the rhythmic outcries of the factions. Thousands of burning tapers waved in a luminous line while down the length of the Mese Way, past the Forum of Constantine and the Capitol Square, the whole court escorted Theodora to her last resting place in the Church of the Holy Apostles.

At the basilica the formal mass for the dead was sung. Again the grand master of ceremonies, approaching the corpse, cried out to it: "Empress, enter into your eternal repose! The King of Kings, the Sovereign of all Sovereigns, calls thee!" Then the marshal lifted the golden diadem from her head and replaced it with a purple band. At last the golden coffin that enclosed the empress's remains was lifted into the great sarcophagus of marble from Hieropolis that she herself had made ready in this Saint Denis of the monarchy. Then the crowd slowly dispersed, and Justinian, crushed with grief, returned with his court to the deserted palace.

When the rest of the empire learned of the death of the redoubtable sovereign, all those who had suffered at her hands experienced a rebirth of their courage and their hopes.

John of Cappadocia hurried to Constantinople, flattering himself that he could regain Justinian's good will. Artabanus, rejecting the wife Theodora had imposed on him, believed the moment had come to be revenged by conspiring against the emperor. Germanus and his sons, extremely excited, thought the hour was right for them to emerge from the long disgrace under which they were clouded. Antonina herself, long the beneficiary of Theodora's friendship, forgot her benefactress and looked for new props for her standing at court.

In the opinion of all, the empress's death would necessarily bring on a reaction both political and religious. Almost at once, the orthodox, scheming at court, were demanding new punishments of the Monophysites, who were terrified by the death of their great protectress. There was talk almost immediately of purging the Sacred Palace of the sacrilegious presence of the monks who had for long sullied the Hormisdas palace. Already Justinian was being urged, since the empress was dead, to force the faith of Chalcedon on those heretics who had falsely procured the favor of the empress and with it dared to resist the emperor's decrees.

All these did not reckon on the deep love that Justinian continued to feel for Theodora, on the long-established habit he had acquired of following her advice, or on the care she had taken before her death to instruct her husband on her supreme wishes and to commend to him all who had loved her and rendered her service. "Desiring," as a contemporary wrote, "to conform, in everything he did, to the wishes of his wife though she was dead," the emperor remained firmly loyal to the counselors with whom she had surrounded herself and to the policy she had laid down.

John of Cappadocia, in spite of his efforts, remained in disgrace. Belisarius, in spite of his honors, remained under suspicion. Peter Barsymes and Narses remained in favor. Antonina, in memory of Theodora's friendship for her, kept the sovereign's confidence. Germanus and his sons were, it is true, restored to favor.

Among the princes in the imperial family, the curopalatin Justin had always been the old emperor's favorite. Theodora had married him to her niece and had designated him the heir presumptive to the monarchy.

In the field of religion, Justinian followed Theodora's instructions with the same fidelity. When the old patriarch Anthimus was discovered in the imperial gynaeceum, where Theodora had concealed him, the emperor gave the heretic prelate a friendly greeting. To everyone's astonishment, the great leaders of Monophysitism—Anthimus, Peter of Apamaeus, Theodosius of Alexandria—were received at the palace as friends. Justinian continued to strive to find with them the means to reestablish peace in the Byzantine church. Until his last day, Justinian tried to carry out the policy of conciliation that Theodora had dreamed of.

Vigilius, mistreated, imprisoned, compelled to flee, finally resigned himself to condemning the "Three Chapters" that the ecumenical council of 553 solemnly anathematized.

To bring back the dissidents, the emperor continued to

arrange discussions and conferences. Though his efforts remained fruitless, he demonstrated the extent to which he remained faithful to Theodora's advice.

Justinian never forgot that fascinating creature, that bold and intelligent partner whom fate had thrown in his path. In memory of her, he wished to keep in his service all those who had been close to her. Until his last day he preserved her memory faithfully. For years, when he had to make a solemn vow, his custom was to swear "by the name of Theodora," and those who wished to please him referred to her as "the excellent, the beautiful and wise sovereign," who, after having been his loyal colleague in this world, was now still praying for him to God.

It must be confessed that this apotheosis is somewhat too fulsome. Theodora the dancer did not exactly possess the virtues that lead straight to paradise. Theodora the empress, in spite of her piety, had faults and vices on which the halo of a saint would not sit too comfortably. But one characteristic is worthy of note. This is that, under the talents of high statecraft that she possessed, this woman of towering ambition always remained all woman and showed, even beyond death, the incomparable potency of her fascination and charm.

Index